AF134832

On Qur'ānic Exegesis

The Great Books of Islamic Civilization
Abridgement Series No.2.

Editorial Board
Aisha al-Mannai, Editor-in-Chief
Dheen Mohamed, Editor
Muhammad Modassir Ali, Editor

The Great Books of Islamic Civilization

On Qur'ānic Exegesis

by

Shaykh Muḥammad Ṭāhir bin 'Āshūr

An abridged English rendering
of the Introductions of
Tafsīr al-Taḥrīr wa al-Tanwīr

by

Muhammad al-Ghazali

Reviewed with a Note by

Dheen Mohamed M. Meerasahib

Edited by

Muhammad Modassir Ali

Foreword

Prof. Aisha Yousef al-Mannai

Director, Center for Muslim Contribution to Civilization

دار جامعة حمد بن خليفة للنشر
HAMAD BIN KHALIFA UNIVERSITY PRESS

Hamad Bin Khalifa University Press
P O Box 5825
Doha, Qatar

www.hbkupress.com

Text Copyright © Muhammad Bin Hamad Al-Thani Center
for Muslim Contribution to Civilization

All rights reserved.

No part of this publication may be reproduced or transmitted in any form or by any means, electronic or mechanical, including photocopying, recording, or any information storage or retrieval system, without prior permission in writing from the publishers.

No responsibility for loss caused to any individual or organization acting on or refraining from action as a result of the material in this publication can be accepted by HBKU Press or the author.

The opinions expressed in this book do not necessarily reflect the opinion of the publisher.

First English edition in 2022

ISBN: 9789927161469

Printed in Doha-Qatar

Qatar National Library Cataloging-in-Publication (CIP)

Ibn ʻĀshūr, Muḥammad al-Ṭāhir, 1879-1973, author.

[تفسير التحرير والتنوير]. Selections. English

On Qur'anic exegesis by Shaykh Muḥammad Ṭāhir ibn ʻĀshūr : an abridged English rendering of the Introductions of Tafsīr al-taḥrīr wa-al-tanwīr / by Muhammad al-Ghazali ; reviewed with Note by Dheen Mohamed M. Meerasahib ; edited by Muhammad Modassir Ali ; forward Prof. Aisha Yousef al-Mannai. First English edition. - Doha, Qatar : Hamad Bin Khalifa University Press, 2022.

pages ; cm. (The Great books of Islamic civilization. Abridgement series. No. 2)

ISBN 978-992-716-146-9

Includes bibliographical references (pages 197-202).

In English; translated from Arabic.

1. Qur'an -- Commentaries -- Early works to 1800. I. Al-Ghazali, Muhammad, translator.
II. Meerasahib, Dheen Mohamed M., reviewer. III. Ali, Muhammad Modassir, editor. IV. Al-Mannai, Aisha Yousef, author of introduction, etc. V. Title.

BP130.4 .I2613 2022
297.1226– dc 23 20222852035x

CONTENTS

MUHAMMAD BIN HAMAD AL THANI CENTER
FOR MUSLIM CONTRIBUTION TO CIVILIZATION 7

FOREWORD 9

REVIEWER'S NOTE 11

INTRODUCTORY REMARKS 17

INTRODUCTORY SECTIONS 41

CHAPTER ONE

Of Exegesis and Hermeneutics; Exegesis being a Science *43*

CHAPTER TWO

Sources of the Science of Tafsīr *51*

CHAPTER THREE

On the Authenticity of Tafsīr without Reliance on Transmitted Reports and the Meaning of Tafsīr based on Opinion *67*

CHAPTER FOUR

What ought to be the Aim of the Mufassir? *85*

CHAPTER FIVE

On the Occasions of Revelation *101*

CHAPTER SIX

Of Recitals *111*

CHAPTER SEVEN

Stories of the Qur'ān *121*

CHAPTER EIGHT

The Names of the Qur'ān, its Chapters, their order and names *129*

8.1. Verses of the Qur'ān........ 133

8.2. Order of Verses........ 138

8.3. Pauses in the Qur'ān........ 143

8.4. Chapters of the Qur'ān 145

CHAPTER NINE

Semantic Scope of the Qur'ān........ *153*

CHAPTER TEN

On the Inimitability of the Qur'ān *163*

10.1. Innovations of the Qur'ān........ 188

10.2. Habits of the Qur'ān 193

Bibliography........ *197*

MUHAMMAD BIN HAMAD AL THANI CENTER FOR MUSLIM CONTRIBUTION TO CIVILIZATION

The Center was established in 1983, when Sheikh Muhammad bin Hamad Al Thani was the Minister of Education for the State of Qatar. The idea behind its formation emerged as a response to the urgent need to provide publication of accurate and academically sound English translations of the most notable works of the Islamic heritage, illustrative of the civilizational and human contribution of Islam, on a global scale.

In May 2010, Her Highness Sheikha Moza bint Nasser, Chairperson of the Qatar Foundation for Education, Science and Community Development announced the affiliation of the Center to the College of Islamic Studies at Hamad bin Khalifa University.

The efforts of the Center were focused almost entirely on translations from Arabic to English language which saw the publication of 16 notable books of the Arab Islamic heritage in 23 volumes all of which related to various disciplines and were published by Garnet Publishing, United Kingdom.

In 2015, the Center reviewed its objectives which now stand as follows:

1. Raising awareness among Muslims and non-Muslims regarding the civilizational heritage of Muslims.
2. Introducing the contributions of Muslims to human civilization.
3. Participating in the promotion of academic research in the area of Islamic civilizational contribution.
4. Enabling researchers in the field of the civilizational contributions of Muslims to communicate and dialogue with each other, with

a view to turning the Center into a bridge and point of collaboration between them.

5. Highlighting and emphasizing the organized endeavors and role of the State of Qatar in the revival of the Islamic civilizational heritage.

In accordance with its objectives, it subsequently expanded the scope of its work and academic pursuits to include:

1. abridgement of a number of significant works
2. editing of manuscripts
3. translation of books from other languages to Arabic and
4. translation of works from English to other world languages.

FOREWORD

I am pleased to introduce to the English-speaking world an abridged version of the Introductions of Muḥammad Ṭāhir bin ʻĀshūr (d. 1393 AH/1973 CE) popularly known as Ibn ʻAshūr to his Tafsir *al-Taḥrīr wa al-Tanwīr*. The Center had so far been publishing translations of classical works of the Islamic civilization. Owing to the expansion of our work's scope, we have now included works which might not be termed classical in the general sense of the word, but which are certainly imbued with that sense of classicism. Ibn ʻĀshūr's *al-Taḥrīr wa al-Tanwīr* is one such work in our estimation, and merited translation into English and publication owing to its comprehensive nature and significance. Qur'ānic studies has long since become an important research area among the Islamists of the West and the modernists of the Muslim world, in addition to its permanently paramount status in the eyes of Muslim scholars.

Al-Taḥrīr wa al-Tanwīr enjoys immense popularity among Muslim scholars and masses, not least because of its engagement with both classical Islamic thought as well as modern reformist thought. No less a reformer himself, Ibn ʻĀshūr's exegesis serves as a convenient bridge between the classical and the modern and provides a breath of fresh air to all those delving in the depths of the Qur'ānic message. His Introduction, popularly known as *Muqaddimat Ibn ʻĀshūr*, beautifully and succinctly weaves all significant issues emerging from the early period of Qur'ānic studies into a narrative that benefits the scholar as much as it does the lay person.

I would like to commend Prof. Muhammad al-Ghazali for rendering this rich text into beautiful English, Prof. Dheen Mohamed of our Center for reviewing the manuscript and penning a Reviewer's note, and Dr. Muhammad Modassir Ali for tirelessly editing the text. I am hopeful that the scholarly community will greatly benefit from this work.

Prof. Aisha al-Mannai

Director, CMCC

REVIEWER'S NOTE

The Muslim world, in recent times, has witnessed the emergence of an increased interest in Qur'ānic studies, especially in its exegetical domain. The interest in itself is not of any surprise, as the Qur'ān – with the Sunnah of the prophet (peace be upon him) – is the foundational source of Islam. Throughout its fourteen centuries of history, no century has passed without some exegetical production of the Qur'ān, usually in the form of commentaries seeing the light of day. Arabic language had the lion's share in this. Although there emerged commentaries in all major Muslim languages, many non-Arab Muslims were also keen to produce their commentaries in Arabic. One of the major motives for this phenomenon was undoubtedly, a sacred affinity that Muslims felt to the Qur'ān and the immense respect in which they held the Arabic language.

Before the dawn of the modern era in the Muslim world, engaging with the Qur'ān through interpretation, exegetical enterprises, scriptural reasoning and other scholarly encounters such as the endeavors to derive legal rulings from it, was considered to be the work of specialized scholars who were recognized by scholarly communities of their time for their competency and excellence in Islamic learning. Their exegetical works displayed their mastery of the knowledge and literary skills needed for such an undertaking. Even those who produced notes on commentaries *(ḥawāshiyy)* such as Tafsīr al-Jamal and al-Ṣāwī, from the Arab world, and Kubra Zadah from among non-Arabs, were experts and accomplished scholars of their times.

With the advent of the modern period in the Muslim world, by the late nineteenth century a radical shift could be observed in the area of Qur'ānic exegesis. A wave of what was termed "reform" slowly started proliferating Muslim consciousness. In some cases it led to a rise in an antagonistic attitude towards the traditional modes of studying the Qur'ān while favoring accommodation of modern western intellectual trends which had started making a niche for themselves throughout the Muslim world. Scholars from Egypt and India, in particular, played a very significant role in this new development and a variety of trends emerged. There were scholars who advocated vehemently against strict adherence to any established school of law and theology. Others began to question the authority of the Sunnah. Still others, motivated by the modernistic spirit, indulged in what they called the modernistic intellectual understanding of the Qur'ān according to which among other things, its miracles became myths and a case for demythologization was made. Still others called for a return to the origins, giving birth to multifarious versions of puritanism. The advocates of all these trends and others felt the necessity of providing a fresh interpretation of the Qur'ān that would help in disseminating their way of seeing Islam and the way forward for Muslims toward progress and development.

In the midst of these concurrently emerging trends and their advocates, the notable presence of an unprecedented conviction loomed large: that direct contact with the Qur'ān and its interpretation did not require knowledge of all those medieval sciences for arriving at a sound understanding of the Qur'ān, and that everyone could and should encounter the Qur'ān directly and without any intermediaries. Many journalistic articles appeared as exegeses of the Qur'ān; many independent *tafsīrs* were produced. Most of them by unqualified people according to the standards set by Muslim intellectual tradition of exegesis. As a result, a type of superficiality started proliferating across the Muslim world concerning Islamic sciences, and most importantly in the area of the Qur'ānic studies.

It is in the midst of these developments that the great Tunisian scholar Muḥammad al-Ṭāhir bin 'Āshūr (d. 1393/1973) appeared as an exceptional scholar. A graduate of al-Zaytūna, Ibn 'Āshūr was an encyclopedic scholar. Like the majority of great Muslim scholars of the past, he excelled in all the major areas of traditional Islamic learning.

He was undoubtedly influenced by the spirit of reform, but his deep knowledge and experience in teaching and writing saved him from falling in the ditch of modernism. He was modern, but not a modernist. It was not easy to avoid the negative influences of the atmosphere of his time, but his mastery of classical sciences, deep insight and wisdom and critical mindset enabled him to maintain a successful balance between competing trends. He wrote many books discussing the Islamic social system, principles of development in Islam, objectives of *sharī'ah* and several monographs, in addition to the countless talks he delivered. His *magnum opus*, however, remains his commentary on the Qur'ān, which he produced in forty-two volumes. In it, Ibn 'Āshūr demonstrates not only his respect for the great classical masters of Qur'ānic scholarship, but one also often finds him critiquing them for what he considers "lapses" on their part and displays a calculated and balanced approach between the scholarship of the past and concerns of his own time. He achieved this balance in a manner that commanded appreciation from all quarters. He did not reduce the Qur'ānic message to a particular notion like some of his contemporaries tended to do. Rather, he took the Qur'ān in its totality and comprehensiveness.

One of the hallmarks of his erudite yet lucid commentary is its introduction. As is usual for many of the lengthy Qur'ānic commentaries of the past, Ibn 'Āshūr's commentary also included in his introduction a lengthy discussion of major issues that pertain to the sciences of the Qur'ān, *'Ulūm al-Qur'ān*. Topics such as the nature of the Qur'ān as a divinely revealed book, its history, message, its collection and transmission, its preservation, its recitations and interpretations are some of the major issues discussed in this introduction. These issues and many others related to them have become the focus of serious interest in western academia only to later resonate in the Arab-Muslim world too. Thus, modern hermeneutics, theories of literary criticism and the various techniques of lower and higher criticism known to the area of biblical criticism have become effective methodological tools in approaching different aspects of the history of the Qur'ān.

Some contemporary western scholars of Qur'ānic studies, such as John Wansbrough, Patricia Crone, Michael Cook and others developed many theories of their own, which their western colleagues themselves found difficult – even impossible – to maintain. Nevertheless, their hypotheses – along with what was already available from the start of the western interest in the Qur'ān, from the Middle Ages in general and from the eighteenth century in particular – constitute an area of concern for contemporary Muslim scholarship.

It is against this background that the CMCC decided to undertake the translation of Ibn 'Āshūr's *Muqaddimah* into English, making available an extraordinary piece of writing on the history of the Qur'ān to scholars of Qur'ānic Studies and adding an indispensable source to those already available for the English-reading scholarly community. It should be remembered that Ibn 'Āshūr does not address a majority of these modern and contemporary issues raised by scholars directly. His discussions of the issues, however, provide concrete material that can help scholars and researchers in the field.

While searching? for a possible translator for this work, we came to know of Prof. Muhammad al-Ghazali's (from the International Islamic University, Islamabad) interest in Ibn 'Āshūr's works. Fortunately for us, he immediately and wholeheartedly accepted our invitation to provide a translation of Ibn 'Āshūr's *Introduction*. Ghazali's abridged translation is preceded by a brief study of the introduction, succinctly summarizing its contents. I had the pleasure of reviewing the translation while its editing and then preparation of the manuscript for publication was carried out by Dr. Muhammad Modassir Ali, Senior Researcher at the Center. It is hoped that this abridged translation will be a welcome addition to the modern library of Qur'ānic Studies and will benefit the scholars of the field.

Finally, I take this opportunity to thank both the translator and the editor for their painstaking work, Prof. Aisha Yousef al-Mannai, Director of the CMCC, for penning the Foreword for this work despite her relentless academic and social engagements. We are particularly indebted to the Hamad Bin Khalifa University Press and their staff for undertaking the publication process of the book with their usual professional excellence.

May Allah bless them all!

Dheen Mohamed
Professor, CMCC at CIS-HBKU
Doha, Qatar
Ramaḍān 1442/April 2021.

INTRODUCTORY REMARKS

Human reason, it is obvious, is not sufficient to answer all questions relating to human felicity and failure. The ultimate moral issues cannot be settled by mere reliance on empirical procedures and rational analyses. Human rational faculties are seldom free from prejudices and subjective predilections, if not obsessions. Deep-seated passions and self-serving emotions also often blur human vision of reality. Religious diversity – present in all periods of history – itself explains these influences on man's quest for self-understanding and ontological awareness. Between pure monotheism and outright polytheism, absolute transcendentalism and total immanentism, notions of unrestrained free will and rigid fatalism, there has appeared in history unlimited variety in religious thought and behavior. These varieties have brought to the fore such a complex and contradictory trajectory of human conception of the sacred and the resultant patterns of religious thought and experience that can provide little help in finding the truth and a straight path to reality.

Ever since his inception in creation, man has pursued the ideal of immortality. Man has struggled hard to find a clue to overcome the phenomenon of death and extinction. A great deal of religious vocation of mankind had been devoted to this apparently impossible aim. They tried to achieve this ideal through finding ways and means of relating themselves to the absolute and the transcendental spheres of the reality. In other words, the search for God was pursued by man as part of his quest for immortality. This aim necessitated an affirmation of afterlife – a life of total emancipation from the ills and imperfections of this world. A great deal of human spiritual endeavor has been directed to this aim. Through pursuing a host of spiritual practices of liberating the self from physical entanglements and animalistic attachments to material and corporeal prisons of this world, man has desperately pursued the ideal of immortality. However, all these endeavors failed to reach the desired aim, if only because these human attempts could not reach the real locus of a true and trustworthy spiritual bond with the Ultimate Reality for want of authentic guidance – a guidance traceable to God and testified by His authorized messengers.

Man has also occupied himself with searching for authentic moral criteria of right and wrong, good and evil in terms of which he could discipline his wayward pursuit of beastly passions and lowly desires. However, groping in darkness without attaining proper guidance by an authentic search has only landed him in contradictions and paradoxes – making history an unending storehouse of ignorance, agnosticism and confusion. Because without an unconditional surrender before a supra-human authority – an authority characterized by (i) absolute knowledge, (ii) total mercy, (iii) complete control over time and space and all existents and (iv) un-mitigated impartiality, all these issues could never be resolved.

Man is not just an animal whose desires and ambitions could be exhausted by mere biological gratification. Hence the endless human quest for religion and spirituality. While physical needs of human life could find means of satisfaction here and now in time-space and the whole environment, the diet of spirit and soul is not obtainable within the physical resources of this habitat. A diet that could quench the thirst of soul and saturate the appetite of the spirit could only be made available from transcendental sources – sources beyond the terrestrial reach of mankind.

A great number of ailments affecting human beings that show themselves in endless anxiety, stress, inner troubles and conflicts, estrangement and ennui that are on the increase despite proliferation in the means of physical pleasure and comfort, is essentially due to lack of proper recourse to the real source of spiritual health and healing. Since these ailments plague the innermost depths of the human soul, these could not find a cure except through the healing touch of the Lord

Creator and hearing His comforting voice expressed in His own Revelation. Any other mode of cure sought elsewhere is of little avail – it is indeed fraught with the greater risk of enhancing the ailment.

There are things visible to the eyes or to the mind's eye, just as there are things that defy these immediate sources of perception. Matters of belief and unbelief, obedience and transgression, good and evil, could only be conceived of through a deeper inner reflection by the heart and soul guided by heavenly light. So physical objects, for instance, need two lights, that of the eye and the outer light of the sun to see. In the same way, the perception of higher realities also requires two lights: the inner light of the soul and the outer light of Divine guidance.

Every human being has an unlimited capacity for love. Love generates the highest urge in man to pursue virtuous and noble aims in life. With the weapon of love, man has been able to conquer everything under the sun. However, all worldly objects of love, being finite, cannot saturate this unlimited capacity for yearning and craving. The ultimate object of love is Allah, the Creator of man and the Generator of love in his life. Love requires knowledge of the beloved. It cannot remain content with ignorance of the beloved. The soul is restless without seeking greater knowledge of the Beloved. This knowledge has been revealed by the Beloved Himself through His Revelation to the one who is His highest loving servant, namely Prophet Muḥammad (peace be upon him).

It is in the nature of man to obey the ordinances issued by those who are worthy of obedience in his estimation. Usually three criteria serve as the key to determine this worth: capacity, generosity and perfection/beauty. The only Being Who stands highest in these three respects is Allah Almighty.

Man by nature is prone to mistakes and blunders as he is inclined to repent and surrender. He errs and repents. He seeks forgiveness and repentance. These are inner matters of the soul beyond penalty and sentence.

There is an inherent moral consciousness present in every human despite all fantastic theories to the contrary. Man cannot exist in an ethical vacuum and moral void. There is no moral holiday in man's life when he could feel emancipated from all scruples. Even if anyone were alone in the wilderness of desert or darkness of ocean, he would still feel the tinge of moral censure over his own acts of evil. Therefore, there has to be somewhere laid down a definitive authoritative moral code to express approval for virtue and disapproval for vice, a code that is clear and transparent to be followed by all. Such a Universal code could only come from a Divine source. Inner consciousness of man demands this code and feels a natural urge to abide by it.

The very existence of man here and now must find a justification, a *raison d'etre*. When man looks around himself, observes and reflects over this vast phenomenon, nothing appears to be without a utility and purpose. He asks himself, muses and wonders about his own place here, his status and vocation. He searches for meaning and purpose of his temporary existence here. His life here in a great many ways is defined in terms of this purpose. Without it, he is at par with this world of matter – the World of bestiality and animality – even worse in utility and status. This purpose could only be defined by Man's Creator and the Creator of the cosmos in which man has been placed. All other explanations are fraught with conflicts and confusions for these have been suggested to man by his own whims and vagaries. The only valid definition of the purpose of creation can come from the Creator Himself. Hence the need for Divine Revelation. If one does acknowledge his Creator and Sustainer, he must also accept Him as a source of Mercy and Compassion. A cursory glance over this universe will provide sufficient evidence for the abundance of Divine Mercy showered all around. Therefore, the Merciful God could not leave His creature alone to grope in the darkness of ignorance regarding his *raison d'etre*. Without a satisfactory answer to this fundamental question by clear Divine Guidance, life could not be immune from moral disaster, spiritual crisis and anarchy.

A book that could serve as the absolute, authentic and trustworthy source of guidance and instruction in all such matters of life in which human reason or imagination are incapable of helping mankind, should be an absolutely true and miraculous book. Otherwise, it will not be able to perform the function of an authentic and trustworthy source of guidance. The Qur'ān is the only such book of guidance that claims to be a true, authentic and inimitable communication from God in absolute terms. It claims to be the only living and valid Divine Speech and Heavenly Guidance for mankind that is available to answer fundamental questions about life and reality. It defines the *raison d'etre* of man in clear and emphatic terms and holds a definite promise of salvation in the hereafter. It lays down eternal laws of ultimate success on the basis of the infinite source of Divine knowledge and wisdom. This Book is not something which might be a result of limited and deficient human intellection or reasoning that is seldom free from subjective feelings, momentary passions, faltering emotions, capricious conceptions or fleeting perceptions. Its laws of moral virtue and rectitude have issued from the Absolute Knowledge of the Creator and Sustainer of mankind who created human nature. This nature is universal and immutable and fully invested by its Creator to cope with the problems and challenges of life through an adequate and adroit moral response under Divine Guidance. For this purpose, sufficient resources have been provided in nature within and nature without. Therefore, pursuing the path laid down in this Book could promise real peace and harmony, justice and balance in life at all levels of existence, because this path has been shown by God who alone is aware of the nature of His own creature, whose will pervades in history and who is observant of all its events.

Over and above this rationale for Divine Guidance – a rationale which springs from undistorted natural reasoning of man, God has invested His Book with internal evidence of its own truth attested by its self-evident miraculous qualities. This has been done to establish a conclusive and incontestable argument for the Divine origin of the Book revealed by Him to His Messenger.

Therefore, the entire credibility of the Qur'ān rests on its uncontested miraculous status, a status that the Qur'ān has forcefully reiterated throughout its pages.

What is a miracle and how it is to be defined in contrast to what is not a miracle?

All things that occur in this world may be classified into three categories: normal events, wonderful events and miraculous events.

The first are events connected with normal cause-effect processes at work in this world of matter, time and space. We sow some seeds in soil and, given necessary conditions, a tree sprouts and yields its fruits. When we fall ill, we take the appropriate medication and relieve ourselves of the pain and suffering from the malady. We feel hunger and satisfy it by proper diet. We undertake trade and commerce and earn profits. We employ various means of overcoming an aggressive enemy in a battle. These are examples of cause-effect processes that are at work in this universe. Our God-given senses and intelligence aid us in knowing and manipulating these processes to our advantage.

The second category consists of certain wonderful and marvelous events. These occur by the use of exceptional knowledge, expertise, ingenuity and imagination wherewith some individuals are specially gifted. In the ultimate analysis, these events are also explainable in terms of the cause-effect system that is operating at a higher plane in the universe. Many inventions by men and women of exceptional talents, including some of the magical wonders, fall in this category. What is common between the first and second categories of events is that a replication is possible in both. Whatever has been achieved by some people could also be attained, even surpassed, by others with more or less similar talent, skill and effort.

But the case of miracles is altogether different. It is an event that takes place in history but it is beyond the reach of historical forces. It cannot be a product of a cause-effect process. It is neither an ordinary occurrence nor even a wonderful event of the second category. It is something that cannot be emulated by mankind's total given capacity. It occurs by Divine Act mediated through the person of the Prophet and manifested through him to humanity at large in space-time. The difference between a miraculous deed and human invention is as wide as the difference between God and man. As man cannot replicate the Divine creation of sun, moon, stars and galaxies, so he is unable to emulate the Divine Miracle. The difference between books produced by human intelligence and ingenuity and the Book revealed by God is infinitely greater. Although God has not explicitly challenged mankind to create the sun and moon, human inability in this regard has been implicitly postulated in the Qur'ān. However, in the case of the Qur'ān, there is an open challenge from its Divine Author, repeated and reiterated in its verses, posed to the entirety of humankind to produce a single specimen similar to its shortest chapter.

No book had been the focus of closer attention by such a large number of learned men throughout such a long time span as the Qur'ān. For the Muslims, this focused interest in the Qur'ān had been quite natural and befitting – an interest that exhausted their potential and resources in reading and understanding this Book. For it represented to them the ultimate source of Divine Guidance and the last call of the Creator to humanity. Even those who failed to recognize its Divine origin could not ignore this Book that changed the entire horizon of human life ever since it entered history. Millions of pages have been written by both believers and non-believers to understand and explain its contents, assess and evaluate its pervasive impact on the course of history. This process is ongoing and would seem set to continue till the end of time. For the believers, it has always been an essential part of their religious life and consciousness. Indeed, for them it will continue to be a part of their reality even beyond the confines of this world. For it has issued from the Divine Attribute of Speech transcending space-time limitations. Authentic Tradition lends credence to the Muslim belief that the Qur'ān will be recited by its own Author as a special rewarding feat to the believers – those inmates of the Paradise who will have endorsed and upheld its eternal truth in this world.

The Muslim undertaking to understand and explain the Qur'ān started with the beginning of its revelation in the seventh century of the Common Era. As the process of revelation continued with the progress of the Prophet's mission of guiding people, forming and reforming the believers' community, the Companions focused their attention on learning and applying the message of the Qur'ān in their lives. The Prophet (peace be upon him) personally presided over this grand activity. He not only communicated every piece of the Revelation to the community – men and women, young and old alike – but also explained its purport and applied its purpose in their lives. He implemented its teachings on himself first, before enforcing its writ on his followers. In this way, the Qur'ān occupied the status of the primary and ultimate source of religious guidance and moral inspiration in the life of the community. At the same time, it became the main generating force of social change and the supreme source of cultural progress and dynamism in the life of the Muslims. The Qur'ān transformed the entire patterns of thought and behavior and the whole spectrum of the lives of its followers. Its reform and education was total and touched every general feature and particular trait of the Muslims' lives. It radically changed perspectives and altered attitudes and animated the Muslim community with a new vision of life and fresh vigor to change the course of history.

Those of the Prophet's Companions who were closest to him were naturally able to receive higher levels of Divine knowledge and wisdom revealed in the Qur'ān as they were greater beneficiaries of its practical fruits of reform and rectitude. There has been from the beginning a close nexus between thought and deed in these Companions' relationship with the Qur'ān. It was this unique integration between knowledge and action engendered in their lives by the Prophet (peace be upon him) that ensured preservation of the Qur'ānic message and its onward transmission. The Companions who carried on the Prophet's mission after him transmitted the knowledge of the Qur'ān – both in theory and practice – to the next generation of the Muslims (*tābi'ūn*). This process, which started in the seventh century of the Common Era, has continued to this day without a moment's interruption. The substance of the Divine Guidance objectified in the Qur'ān was essentially supplied by the teaching of the Prophet (peace be upon him) who exemplified its ideal application as the highest model of Islamic vision and values. Those of his Companions who directly benefited from him, passed on this legacy to the younger generations of the Muslims. In this way, not only the text of the Revelation was preserved by the community but also its authentic explanation. This authentic explanation was provided by the Prophet (peace be upon him) and those of his Companions who attended the events of the Revelation and practically participated in the reform initiated by the Qur'ān under the Prophet's leadership and guidance.

This, however, does not mean that human reason has been barred from pondering and reflecting on the Qur'ān because the Prophet (peace be upon him) had already supplied its authentic interpretation. On the contrary, the latter served as a basic guiding framework for a continuous study and understanding of the Divine Book by the subsequent generations of the Muslims. Within the given framework of meaning and purpose and without prejudice to the authentic principles of interpretation, the scholars of Islam have exhausted their potential to study the Qur'ān, enrich and expand, deepen and diversify its knowledge. These efforts gradually contributed to the crystallization of the distinct discipline of *tafsīr*. The various approaches adopted by the scholars of *tafsīr* in understanding and explicating the Qur'ānic text further diversified this core discipline into different branches – all focused on discerning the Divine will as revealed in the Qur'ān.

Apart from various branches of *tafsīr* that grew out of the main tree, as it were, like legal, linguistic and literary studies of the Qur'ān, another important field of study gradually evolved which was given the name: *'Ulūm al-Qur'ān*. The latter was in fact an enlarged form of introduction to *tafsīr* that constituted integral part of major works of *tafsīr*. It covered those features of the Qur'ān, the knowledge of which was regarded as necessary to the understanding of the Qur'ān or more specifically to the study of *tafsīr*. The field of *'Ulūm al-Qur'ān* had been increasingly expanding during the last one hundred years encompassing mainly the following topics related to *tafsīr*. (i) Revelation: history, stages, compilation and recording, variant readings, order of verses and chapters etc., and (ii) Inimitability of the Qur'ān: various concepts of the miracle, Arabs' response to the Qur'ān, different views about rhetorical aspects of the Qur'ān, literary evidence of the Qur'ānic miracle etc.

These aspects of knowledge about the Qur'ān have been regarded as essential introduction to the study of the *tafsīr* proper. In recent times, *'Ulūm al-Qur'ān* has been incorporated as a regular part of the curricular scheme of Islamic education giving the discipline a new momentum and serving as an incentive to greater academic activity in the field.

In the tradition of scholarship on *tafsīr*, the greatest Muslim geniuses of all ages have made a significant contribution toward enriching this field. Through the development of the discipline of *tafsīr* these great scholars have participated in this historical project without interruption since the Prophet's time. Each writer on *tafsīr* has, in a way, presented to posterity all the fruits of his labor of love, expressed in the form of reflection on the Divine Book, an occupation that virtually claims life-long engagement. In addition to this enthusiastic participation by the most celebrated scholars of the community, in explaining and spreading the message of the Qur'ān, many of the scholars of *tafsīr* have also shared with their readers the highlights of the long path of the struggle made by them to reach an understanding of the Qur'ān. As pointed out above, they rendered this service to their readers in the form of their comprehensive prologues to *tafsīr*.

Each of these introductions varies in size, scope and volume. While most of them are concise and focused on the salient features of this discipline, briefly outlining the approach adopted in their own works, some are quite copious and comprehensive. Such lengthy prologues contain elaborate introductions to the discipline of *tafsīr*. This is in addition to explaining at length the manner in which they dealt with the issues involved in the works produced by them. In this way, such introductions assume the status of a full-fledged monograph on the grammar of *tafsīr*, as it were. One of the outstanding specimens of such a comprehensive introduction in the recent times, is the one written by Ibn 'Āshūr.[1]

Muḥammad al-Ṭāhir bin 'Āshūr, the author of this work on *tafsīr*, was born in Tunisia in 1879 and died there in 1973. His family, especially his father Muḥammad and his maternal grandfather Muḥammad al-'Azīz bin 'Atūr, had been highly reputed for religious scholarship. This scholarly background provided a conducive atmosphere for the exceptional academic growth and development of Muḥammad al-Ṭāhir bin 'Āshūr.

His early education started by memorizing the Qur'ān. This was followed by a study based on the curricular textbooks of Islamic disciplines. At the young age of fourteen, he joined the famous seminary of al-Zaytūna for advanced studies in Islamic disciplines. He proved himself a bright student in completing the courses of study at al-Zaytūna covering the disciplines of *sharī'ah*, Arabic language and literature, medicine and French language.

The well-known works of Ibn 'Āshūr include, apart from the present work on *tafsīr*, *Maqāṣid al-Sharī'ah*, *Uṣūl al-Niẓām al-Ijtimā'ī fī al-Islām*, *Uṣūl al-Taqaddum fī al-Islām* and many others including some unpublished works. In his writings, Ibn 'Āshūr has been recognized by his contemporaries as a profound author treating the subject from a rich multi-disciplinary background. The scholars of Tunisia regard him as the last specimen of the all-round classical scholarship of yore. This trait is reflected, among other things, in his mastery of Arabic prose, something that has been seen as reminiscent of the great stylists of the past.

---

1 The biographical information about Ibn 'Āshūr has been taken from *Madkhal li Tafsīr al-Taḥrīr wa al-Tanwīr li Ibn 'Āshūr* by Muḥammad bin Ibrāhīm al-Ḥamad.

Muhammad Ṭāhir al-Mīsāwī, a contemporary scholar from Tunisia, sums up his estimation of the vast academic potential of Ibn 'Āshūr in the following words: "his life is so rich and varied in academic attainments that little wonder when you go through any of his works, you feel as if you were in the company of a galaxy of scholars combining a linguist, a man of letters, an exegete, a doctor of the tradition, jurist, educationist, historian, philosopher and logician." This eulogistic sort of statement by al-Mīsāwī might smack of the exaggeration of many modern intellectuals who are prone to perceive knowledge as necessarily classified into given categories of so-called specialization. But those of us who have had the good fortune of seeing some recent intellectual masters and pedagogists of the traditional lore – men who could still be found living until the 80s and 90s of the previous century – though they were by then fast becoming a rare breed and scarce resource – will easily testify to the accuracy of his estimation and veracity of his appreciation.

However, according to most of his biographers and reviewers, his vast understanding in the whole range of the traditional Islamic learning apart, Ibn 'Āshūr stands out prominently as an exceptional scholar of *tafsīr* as fully borne out by his work *al-Taḥrīr wa al-Tanwīr*.

He has attempted this *tafsīr*, his *magnum opus*, from the strength of possessing a vast understanding of the main currents in the prevailing tradition of Islamic scholarship. He thus put his life-long earnings in the studies of Islam at the service of his exegetical project.

This present work is an abridged English translation of the author's long introduction to the outstanding work of *Tafsīr*: *al-Taḥrīr wa al-Tanwīr*. This introduction is so comprehensive and well-written that it contains elements of a full-fledged work on *'Ulūm al-Qur'ān*. It agitates more or less the same conventional issues that formed the substance of earlier works albeit with many variations on the theme and useful additions to the subject.

This comprehensive introduction has been divided by the author into ten sections, each dealing with an important issue concerning *tafsīr*. A precis of each section is provided below.

(i) In section one, the author has discussed the literal and technical meanings associated with the key words *tafsīr* and *ta'wīl*. Defining the science of *tafsīr*, he says: "it is the name of that discipline which discusses the meanings of the Qur'ānic words and the brief or extensive knowledge derived therefrom." He, however, points out that using the word "science" (*'ilm*) for *tafsīr* is a liberal application of the term. He justifies this application by registering the fact that Muslim scholars engaged themselves with this field of knowledge before developing other Islamic disciplines. Scholastic pursuit of *tafsīr* by the early scholars engendered among them the skill of discerning the peculiar features of Qur'ānic discourse. Their insights were disseminated among the later scholars of the Qur'ān, who found them immensely beneficial in their studies and placed them prominently in their written notes on *tafsīr*. These notes gradually evolved into a systematic and organized knowledge about the Qur'ān. In this way, a distinct discipline emerged which was focused on knowledge of the Qur'ān. The author has also explained in this section, the status of *tafsīr* in the whole body of Islamic knowledge called *al-'Ulūm al-Shar'iyyah*, placing it at the head for obvious reasons.

He has also traced the genesis of *tafsīr* to the earliest periods of the revelation. After highlighting the seminal contribution made by two prominent Companions, namely 'Abd Allāh bin 'Abbās and 'Alī bin Abī Ṭālib, to the foundation of *tafsīr*, he cautions against many weak and unauthentic reports that have crept into certain works of *tafsīr* claiming their origin in the statements of these two Companions.

Further, in this section, the author has explained the linguistic and technical difference between the terms *tafsīr* and *ta'wīl*.

Citing various usages of these terms as mutually distinct – even exclusive– that have been in vogue among some scholars, he takes the position that essentially the two terms are interchangeable.

(ii) In this section, the author explains the main sources of knowledge on which scholars of *tafsīr* must rely in order to qualify for a scholarly study of *tafsīr*. These sources, according to him, include thorough knowledge of Arabic language, including a profound understanding of Rhetoric and Stylistics. The author cites earlier authorities, like al-Zamakhsharī and al-Sakkākī, to emphasize the essential requirement of a deep awareness of the literary tradition of Arabic language in order to appreciate the inimitable character of the Qur'ān. In fact, he goes further than this to argue that a knowledge of the linguistic and literary aspects of the Qur'ānic text is a *sine qua non* even for deriving injunctions from its verses. He cites a number of verses to substantiate this argument by demonstrating that the real stress, emphasis, purport, purpose or implication of a Qur'ānic statement could only be appreciated by recourse to the above fields of knowledge. For without reference to the canons of Arabic Rhetoric and Stylistics, the definite import of a Divine statement could hardly be determined in terms of approval and disapproval. And without the latter, no injunctions could be derived from the Qur'ān and, therefore, the Divine will cannot be revealed to the human mind.

(iii) The third section deals with a highly important and sensitive issue relating to *tafsīr*, namely the status of "received knowledge" or the explanation of the Qur'ān based on reports (*al-Ma'thūr*) and its counterpart, namely the knowledge of the Qur'ān based on individual thinking or opinion (*al-Ra'y*). The author discusses various views in this regard. After a critical evaluation of these views, he comes to the conclusion that very little substantial *tafsīr* is traceable to the Prophet (peace be upon him). Whatever quantum of knowledge relating to the Qur'ān that has been handed down by the Companions had been, according to the author, in the nature of personal views of these Companions deduced from the Qur'ān. To support this view, the author refers to variant reports of *tafsīr* traceable to different Companions. If all these explanations of Qur'ānic verses were based on the Prophet's authoritative interpretation, he argues, then there should have been no variance in these reports. This fact has led the author to the conclusion that while certain portions, albeit highly significant ones, have been interpreted by the Prophet (peace be upon him) himself, the rest of the Companions' reports of *tafsīr* fall in the category of individual reflection on the Qur'ān and the fruits of this reflection. Therefore, the author asserts, the field of *tafsīr* must essentially be a synthesis of both the elements of reason (*al-Ra'y*) and tradition (*al-Ma'thūr*).

Thereafter, the author agitates the issue of the so-called esoteric interpretation of the Qur'ān. He explains the problem with reference to the seminal contribution of Imam Ghazālī to this subject. The latter not only critically examined this trend but also presented, in his own writings, the valid form of such an extended interpretation. The author notes, in the light of Imam Ghazālī's criticism of this trend, the damage done by its votaries to the comprehensibility of the Qur'ān. He cites a number of examples from the texts of the Qur'ān to demonstrate the difference between the two kinds of esoteric interpretation: admissible and inadmissible. The first maintains the original direct meaning of the text but transcends it to derive a moral lesson relevant for the present reader. The second undermines the exoteric message of the Qur'ān in preference for the so-called inner and occult nuances.

According to the author, the modes and methods of interpreting the Qur'ānic text developed and defined by the scholars of *tafsīr* provide sufficient security against any such distortive attempts.

(iv) In section four, the author defines the aims that a competent scholar of the Qur'ān should pursue. In this context, he spells out the fundamental objectives of Revelation to emphasize the need for a *mufassir* to function within the framework of these objectives. A conscious observance of these objectives on the part of the scholar shall guard him against rendering the text as a fluid open-ended object of reading into it whatever runs contrary to its real objectives. He frequently cites verses from the Qur'ān – in both this and other sections – to underline a strict adherence to this purposeful pursuit of Qur'ānic study. For to him, no amount of scholarly activity or ratiocination focused on the Qur'ān could yield any meaningful fruit if it vitiates the very objectives that this Book so clearly defines for itself. In this respect, the author spells out the following objectives of the Revelation:

1. reforming beliefs and teaching the right creed;
2. reforming morals;
3. general and particular injunctions;
4. defining the political order of the *Ummah*;
5. narrating events of past peoples and communities;
6. teaching people in accordance with the needs of the time;
7. preaching and counseling, giving glad tidings and admonitions; and
8. establishing evidence for the inimitability of the Qur'ān.

Thereafter, he defines the scope of *tafsīr* and points to various approaches – both general and specific – adopted by different scholars in their works. He also determines the limits for bringing the discussion of various issues pertaining to other branches of Islamic studies into the works of *tafsīr*. In this respect, he clearly places various other Islamic disciplines in relation to the discipline of *tafsīr* to show how far a *mufassir* could be justified in expanding his discussion with the help of the other disciplines. In sum, he concludes that any piece of knowledge or insight provided by other disciplines that is helpful in understanding the import and implications of Qur'ānic verses could profitably be included in the discussions of *tafsīr*. In this regard, the author notices two different trends among the scholars of Islam. One of them, represented by Ibn Rushd (junior), is the attempt to demonstrate a concord and compatibility between the statements of the Qur'ān and the findings of human knowledge relevant to those statements. The author has recorded his own preference for this trend. However, he has laid down certain conditions for this enlargement of the framework of *tafsīr*: (i) extreme brevity in the mention of issues relating to other branches of knowledge; (ii) strict adherence to Arabic semantics in deducing meanings from the Qur'ānic text that are related to other branches of knowledge; (iii) maintaining the direct literal sense of the words and constructions unless there is a strong reason to make a departure from it; (iv) avoiding any attempt to press into service a meaning artificially – a meaning contrary to the direct spontaneous connotation supported by Arabic semantics.

The other trend is represented by men like al-Shāṭibī and Abū Bakr bin al-'Arabī. They held that the quantum of knowledge available to the early Arabs had been sufficient for the comprehension of the Qur'ānic message. Any subsequent development and expansion in human knowledge, therefore, need not be relied upon to interpret the statements of the Qur'ān, they argued. The author, however, strongly refutes this argument and contends that though essential guidance had been available to the early generations from the Qur'ānic text, findings and insights from other sources could subsequently become available which could help a *mufassir* attain a better understanding and application of the text. He also expresses the view that many of these insights, independently attained by men of knowledge, could lend further evidence to the truth of the Qur'ān and thus testify to its miraculous status. The author, however, admits that indeed there remain many areas of human knowledge and experience that have little connection with the Qur'ān, like mythology, prosody and rhymes etc. Therefore, he concludes, such things as provide no aid in our understanding of the Revelation fall outside the scope of *tafsīr*.

(v) Section five has been devoted to a discussion of the occasions of the revelation (*asbāb al-nuzūl*). Ibn 'Āshūr points out that often these receive exaggerated attention to the extent that it seems that each verse must necessarily have been revealed in connection with a historical event. However, the fact of the matter, according to the author, is that the Qur'ān, which has been revealed for the guidance of humanity, does not depend for its unfolding in history on any incident requiring particular legislation. Yet indeed, the author contends, there are certain occasions that should be known to a scholar of *tafsīr* if only because they relate to a verse in many significant ways. These either provide detail for some concise expression, elaborate some ambiguous statement or explicate the content from any other aspect. There are also certain occasions that may guide a scholar to the arguments relevant to the explanation of a verse, or to the appreciation of some rhetorical aspects of the Qur'ān. Since appreciating the literary miracle of the Qur'ān depends on an acute knowledge about the circumstances attending the revelation, a knowledge of these occasions is extremely significant for this purpose.

The author classifies these occasions into five main categories:

1. where understanding of a verse, which is ambiguous, depends on the understanding of the occasion;
2. where a historical event gives rise to certain revelation;
3. where many events occur in succession. Then a verse is revealed containing an injunction. When the scholars say that this verse has been revealed concerning that event, they only mean that this particular event/individual is included in the application of this verse.
4. where some verses have an apparent connection with some events. When a scholar points out this connection, it seems as if these verses are meant to refer to these events per se. However, the aim of the scholar is only to point to the fact that these events are included in the general message contained in these verses;
5. where these occasions help explain certain ambiguities that appear in some of the verses;

The author has illustrated these five categories with examples from the Qur'ān to show the valid use of the occasions of the revelation. There seem, however, to be striking similarities between some of the above categories, particularly between the first and the fifth and between the third and the fourth. Therefore, these could easily be reduced to three categories rather than five.

(vi) In section six, the author discusses the variant readings of the Qur'ān. He points out that this variance is of two categories, one of which has no relation to the study of *tafsīr*. Therefore, he discusses in this section only that category which has relevance for *tafsīr*.

The sum total of the author's discussion is that in the reading of the Qur'ān with variant modes – all approved by the Prophet (peace be upon him) – there is yet more evidence of the rich linguistic resources of this Book. For these variant readings often supply an abundance of meaning. In this way, the author contends, the semantic expanses of the Qur'ān are further widened.

He sums up the discussion about the authenticity of variant readings of the Qur'ān by stating that any modes of reading which are in accord with the standard usage of Arabic, the Master-Script of 'Uthmān (may God be pleased with him) and are established by an overwhelming chain of transmitters (*mutawātir*) are valid. He also mentions at some length the series of events in the development of the Qur'ānic script since the beginning of the revelation leading to its culmination in the preparation of the Master-Script by 'Uthmān. He registers the fact that the majority of the variant readings are in accordance with the Master-Script. He cites a number of telling examples to illustrate this concordance.

(vii) In section seven, the author talks about an important Qur'ānic theme, namely the stories of the past peoples. He discusses the relevance of these stories to the supreme objectives of the Revelation already identified by him in the previous sections. He invites the reader's attention to the peculiar Qur'ānic style in narrating these stories. He shows how these narrations, which are mentioned piecemeal and intermittently in different chapters, are linked to the theme of preaching, reminding and counselling—a theme of central importance in the Qur'ān. He also elaborates on the subtle rhetorical qualities of the Qur'ān as reflected in its narrative style.

(viii) In the eighth section, the author talks about the various attributive names of the Qur'ān—names that are derived from the text itself such as *al-Kitāb*, *al-Furqān*, *al-Dhikr* and *al-Waḥy*. Also included in this section is an explanation of the names of the chapters in the Qur'ān and the order of the verses. He defines the basic unit of the Qur'ānic text, namely the Verse, and talks at some length about the criteria of delimiting the verses of the Qur'ān. He points out that this delimitation is based on the authoritative command of the Prophet (peace be upon him) and is not subject to the choice of those Companions who recorded the text under the Prophet's guidance, 'Uthman (may God be pleased with him) included. The Companions, the author notes, had been familiar with this basic division of the Divine text throughout, since it was laid down by the Prophet (peace be upon him). The author also explains the difference and commonality that is found between the endings of the verses and the terminal pauses. The latter are an important feature of the rhetorical qualities of the Qur'ān. However, these terminal pauses (*fawāṣil*), which often coincide with the endings of verses, should be distinguished from simple pauses that are placed in the text as signs to take a breath during recital.

Concerning the order maintained in the Qur'ān by the authoritative command of the Prophet (peace be upon him) (*tawqīf*), the author emphasizes the point that this order is a unique feature of the Qur'ān that has an inseparable link to the inimitability of the Qur'ān. Therefore, any slight alteration in this order must always be at the expense of the miraculous status of the Divine Book.

According to the author, at all stages of the recording of the Scripture since the Prophet's own time up to the era of the third Caliph 'Uthmān, there had been a consensus among all the Companions—the first two Caliphs included—that this was indeed the correct order of the verses of the Qur'ān. The same order was also maintained by the members of the early Muslim community in their recitation of the Qur'ān, on the basis of what they heard from the Prophet (peace be upon him) himself during the twenty-three years of his life as a Prophet. At the same time, the author takes notice of some reports that imply the existence of written parts of the Qur'ān with some of the Companions, in which a different order of the chapters is to be found. He explains this variation by saying that certain Companions had been preparing their own copies of what they learnt of the Qur'ān from time to time. Since the Qur'ān was revealed in parts, it is probable that they missed some revealed text-verses or chapters; hence the discrepancy. Apart from this exception, the scripts prepared by those Companions who were chosen by the Prophet (peace be upon him) as his official scribes of the Revelation followed the same order as was determined by the Prophet (peace be upon him) based on the Divine Command. In the same section, the author also discusses the names of the chapters that have been designated by the Prophet (peace be upon him) himself or by the Companions with his tacit approval. In this connection, he shows the link between these names and the contents of the chapters.

(ix) In section nine, the author discusses the semantic expanses of the Qur'ānic text. Citing examples from the Qur'ān, he shows that there are profuse instances of employing a single word or construction for multiple connotations – all signified expressly or implied tacitly at once. At the same time, these examples are in accord with the linguistic usage of the Arabs that was in vogue among the addressees of the Qur'ān. The author cites a number of examples where a single word employed in the Qur'ān carries different meanings in the Arabs' usage and all of them are intended simultaneously in the Qur'ān. He also shows that the Qur'ān at times employs one word in both its literal sense and in the metaphorical meaning. He points out the fact that the scholars of Islamic Jurisprudence have also dealt with this issue and adopted different views about it. He personally advocates the view taken by the Shāfi'ī school in the matter that supports the possibility of extensive and varied connotations carried by certain words or constructions in the Qur'ān. According to him, this wide scope of Qur'ānic semantics provides yet further evidence of the linguistic miracle of the Qur'ān.

(x) In the last section of his introduction, the author has discussed the miraculous status of the Qur'ān in some detail. In line with the consensus of the Muslim scholars, he holds that the real basis of the miraculous nature of the Qur'ān is its inimitable perfection in the scales of linguistic, rhetorical, and stylistic qualities. The author identities three main dimensions of the Qur'ānic miracle:

1. highest summit of subtle literary sublimity;
2. innovation in rhetorical communication and stylistic harmony unattained by the Arabs before the revelation of the Qur'ān or after it;
3. introducing such wealth of knowledge that had been beyond the reach of human experience, reason or imagination.

According to the author, the main addressees of the first two of these dimensions had been primarily the Arabs and those non-Arabs who might attain the same high standards of linguistic skill and literary judgment that had been the hallmark of the early Arabs. While the third dimension is applicable to all mankind. The author, at the same time, emphasizes the fact, as also pointed out by a number of scholars before him, that for the non-Arabs of all times too, the Qur'ān constitutes a literary miracle in that they are well aware of the failure of the Arabs to counter the Qur'ānic challenge of emulating a single chapter of it. This despite the compulsion that the adversaries of the Prophet (peace be upon him) felt to combat the mission of the Prophet (peace be upon him). These Arab adversaries of the Prophet (peace be upon him), especially his contemporaries, chose to face great hardships of war and armed conflict in their bid to defeat him and his reforms, but did not pursue the far easier peaceful path of confronting the literary challenge of the Qur'ān. This fact of history furnishes unmistakable evidence of their acknowledged defeat in the face of this Qur'ānic challenge. As the author has mentioned in section II of his introduction, a profound knowledge of this miraculous status of the Qur'ān is a *sine qua non* for anyone who wishes to undertake a scholarly study of the Qur'ān.

As will have become clear from the foregoing remarks of the translator, this introduction to the exegetical work *al-Taḥrīr wa al-Tanw*īr by Shaykh Ṭāhir bin 'Āshūr is full of useful information and insights about *tafsīr*. Hence our decision to share its useful contents with English-speaking readers unable to benefit from the original Arabic work. We hope that our decision will be vindicated by a fruitful addition to the scanty material available in English on *'Ulūm al-Qur'ān*.

Finally, I acknowledge with thanks the help rendered by Dr. Muhammad Islam, Research Associate/Lecturer at the Islamic Research Institute, in writing these remarks and in providing documentation for the works cited in the Introduction by Ibn 'Āshūr. I would also like to acknowledge that I have benefited immensely from *'Ulūm al-Qur'ān* by late Mawlānā Shams al-Ḥaq Afghānī, a scholar of great renown from Pakistan.

Muhammad al-Ghazali

INTRODUCTORY SECTIONS

CHAPTER ONE

OF EXEGESIS AND HERMENEUTICS; EXEGESIS BEING A SCIENCE

Tafsīr (Exegesis) is an infinitive (verbal noun) of the verb: *fassara*, with an accentuated *sīn* (s). The latter is a multiplied form *(muḍā'af)* of the verb *fasara*, without accent on the *sīn*. This verb belongs to the group of verbs known as *naṣara* and *ḍaraba*. The verbal noun of this verb is *fasr*. Both of them are transitive verbs. Therefore, the accent is not meant to convey transitiveness.

The word *fasr* means to reveal and unveil the intended meaning of a speech or word by means of another phrase which is clearer in meaning in the mind of the listener than the speech or the word intended to be explained.

Further, it has been said that the two verbal nouns or verbs are identical in meaning. It has also been opined that a multiplied verb (*muḍā'af*) is meant for explaining intellectual issues. This has been held by al-Rāghib and the author of *al-Baṣā'ir*.[1] It seems that this opinion is based on the idea that a statement of intellectual issues involves excess of speech on the part of the one who explains them.

This explanation is supported by the verse of the Qur'ān 25:33 "And they come not to thee with any parable, but that We bring to thee the truth and a better explanation."

This verb, when it is multiplied (*muḍā'af*) to convey a sense of transitiveness, also delivers an allied meaning of augmentation. That is

---

1 Abū al-Qāsim al-Ḥusayn bin Muḥammad al-Rāghib al-Aṣfahānī, *al-Mufradāt fī Gharīb al-Qur'ān*, Muḥammad Sayyid Kaylānī, ed. (Beirut: Dār al-Ma'rifah, n.d.), 380; Muḥammad bin Ya'qūb al-Fayrūz Ābāḍī, *Baṣā'ir Dhawī al-Tamyīz fī Laṭā'if al-Kitāb al-'Azīz*, Muḥammad 'Alī al-Najjār, ed. (Beirut: Dār al-Kutub al-'Ilmiyyah, n.d.), 4: 192.

why ‘Allāmah al-Zamakhsharī said in the opening lines of his work *al-Kashshāf*, “praise is due to God who sent down the Qur’ān as a well-organized and composed speech and sent it down piecemeal according to the weal.”[1] The scholars who have written commentaries on his work have remarked that he (i.e. al-Zamakhsharī) has combined the two verbal forms, (one without accent and another with accent i.e. *Anzala* and *Nazzala*) because the latter verb carries a sense of augmentation.[2]

In the technical sense, *tafsīr* (Exegesis) stands in our view for: “the discipline that discusses the explanation of the meaning of the words of the Qur’ān and whatever is understood from them briefly or in detail.” The connection between the literal and technical meanings of this word is self-evident and, therefore, does not require any elaboration.

The subject matter of *tafsīr* are the words of the Qur’ān in terms of their meanings and what is derived therefrom. In this aspect, it excludes the science of recitals. Because the distinction of a discipline is determined by the distinction of its subject matter and the perspective from which it is dealt with.

However, to regard *tafsīr* as a science *(‘ilm)* is a liberal application of the term. But the scholars of Islam have done it in view of the fact that this discipline is based on certain basic premises and principles that serve as a foundation for deriving the meaning of the Qur’ānic text and interpreting the Qur’ānic verses. Otherwise, in the sense in which the term science is employed for rational sciences, this term does not seem to apply to *tafsīr*. Also a great deal of discussion that takes place in the works of *tafsīr* leads to the deduction of abundant knowledge and general principles. These principles should be seen as on par with

---

1 Maḥmūd bin ‘Umar al-Zamakhsharī, *al-Kashshāf ‘an Ḥaqā’iq Ghawāmiḍ al-Tanzīl wa ‘Uyūn al-Aqāwīl fī Wujūh al-Ta’wīl*, henceforth, *al-Kashshāf*, ‘Ādil Aḥmad ‘Abd al-Mawjūd and ‘Alī Muḥammad Mu‘awwaḍ, eds. (Riyadh: Maktabat al-‘Abīkān, 1418/1998), 1: 95.

2 Al-Sayyid al-Sharīf ‘Alī bin Muḥammad bin ‘Alī al-Ḥusaynī al-Jurjānī, *al-Ḥāshiyah ‘alā Kitāb al-Kashshāf* (n.p.: Sharikat Maktabat wa Maṭba‘at Muṣṭafā al-Bābī al-Ḥalabī wa Awlāduh, 1385/1966), 3-4.

the basic logical principles that underlie the rational sciences. Similarly, the scholars have regarded stylistics and prosody as sciences although these only form definitions of certain technical terms adopted in these branches.

Since this discipline aims to state and explain the Divine intent in His speech, it is to be regarded among the foundational disciplines of the *sharīʻah*. Indeed it occupies the status of head of these disciplines as pointed out by al-Bayḍāwī also.[1]

Historically, *tafsīr* was also the first of the Islamic disciplines to emerge. Deep reflection on the Qur'ān had started at the time of the Prophet (peace be upon him). Some Companions of the Prophet (peace be upon him) asked him about the meaning of some verses. For example, 'Umar (may God be pleased with him) asked the Prophet (peace be upon him) about *kalālah* (those who leave no ascendants or descendants as heirs).[2] Thereafter, among the Companions, 'Alī (may God be pleased with him) and Ibn 'Abbās (may God be pleased with him) rose to great fame in the field of *tafsīr* as these two spoke about *tafsīr* more than others; also rising to prominence in this field were Zayd bin Thābit, Ubayy bin Ka'b, 'Abd Allāh bin Mas'ūd and 'Abd Allāh bin 'Amr bin al-'Āṣ (may God be pleased with them). When people who were not native speakers of the Arabic language entered the fold of Islam, deliberation over the Qur'ān increased. This fact necessitated the task of explaining the meaning of the Qur'ān to these newcomers. In time of the generation who came after that of the Companions (*tābiʻūn*), this knowledge (of *tafsīr*) was further disseminated. Those who rose to prominence in this period include Mujāhid and Ibn Jubayr. Thus this discipline is the most auspicious of – and is rightly regarded as the head of – all Islamic sciences.

---

1 'Abd Allāh bin 'Umar bin Muḥammad al-Shīrāzī al-Bayḍāwī, *Anwār al-Tanzīl wa Asrār al-Ta'wīl al-Ma'rūf bi Tafsīr al-Bayḍāwī*, henceforth, *Anwār al-Tanzīl* (n.p.: Dār al-Jīl, 1329 AD), 2.

2 Muslim bin al-Ḥajjāj bin Muslim al-Qushayrī, *Ṣaḥīḥ Muslim* (Riyadh: Dār al-Salām, 1419/1998), 706, ḥadīth no. 4150.

The first person to write on *tafsīr* was 'Abd al-Malik bin Jurayj al-Makkī (born in 80 AH and died in 149).[1] He wrote his book on the *tafsīr* of numerous verses. He also collected it in many reports. Mostly he narrates from the disciples of Ibn 'Abbās like 'Aṭā' and Mujāhid. Many works of *tafsīr* also appeared with reports attributed to Ibn 'Abbās. However, the scholars of tradition expressed criticism of them. For example, Muḥammad bin al-Sā'ib al-Kalbī's *tafsīr* (d. 146 AH) is based on reports by one Abū Ṣāliḥ from Ibn 'Abbās. The latter had been accused of uttering falsehoods to the extent of earning the title of *Darawgh zan* (liar).[2] And indeed the reports collected in the above work are the weakest reports. If the narrations of Muḥammad bin Marwān al-Suddī on the authority of al-Kalbī are added to them, then it will be a "chain of lies".[3] What the scholars meant by this appellation is that it is the opposite of what they have considered "the golden chain" comprising of Mālik to Nāfi' to Ibn 'Umar. It has also been reported that the aforementioned al-Kalbī was among the followers of 'Abd Allāh bin Saba'. The latter was of Jewish origin and had entered Islam but used to defame the first three Caliphs. However, he expressed excessive reverence for 'Alī bin Abī Ṭālib. He also claimed that 'Alī had not died and would come back to this world. It has been reported that he also claimed divinity for 'Alī.[4]

There are also narrations of Muqātil, Ḍaḥḥak and 'Alī bin Abī Ṭalḥah al-Hāshimī, all from Ibn 'Abbās. The most authentic of them is the narration of 'Alī bin Abī Ṭalḥah. Bukhārī has relied on the latter in the 'book of *tafsīr* in his *Ṣaḥīḥ*. The author of *al-Itqān* has produced all these reports narrated by Bukhārī from Alī bin Abī Talḥah on the

1 Muḥammad bin 'Alī bin Aḥmad al-Dāwūdī, *Ṭabaqāt al-Mufassirīn* (Beirut: Dār al-Kutub al-'Ilmiyyah, n.d.), 1: 358-59.

2 Muḥammad bin Aḥmad al-Qurṭubī, *al-Jāmi' li Aḥkām al-Qur'ān*, Ṣadqī Muḥammad Jamīl and 'Irfān al-'Ashshā, eds. (Beirut: Dār al-Fikr, 1414/1993), 1: 1: 42.

3 Jalāl al-Dīn 'Abd al-Raḥmān al-Suyūṭī, *al-Itqān fī 'Ulūm al-Qur'ān*, henceforth, *al-Itqān*, Muṣṭafā Dīb al-Bughā, ed. (Beirut: Dār Ibn Kathīr, 1407/1987), 2: 1232.

4 Khayr al-Dīn al-Ziriklī, *al-A'lām*, 5th ed. (Beirut: Dār al-'Ilm li al-Malāyīn, 1980), 4: 88, 6: 133.

authority of Ibn ‘Abbās. He has arranged them all according to the order of the chapters in the Qur’ān.

In short, the fabricators have taken refuge in the narrations from Ibn ‘Abbās to claim authenticity for whatever they desired like all other people who attribute anonymous reports and anecdotes to the most famous person in the field.

There are also narrations attributed to ‘Alī bin Abī Ṭālib (may God be pleased with him), most of which are fabricated, except those that have been transmitted through a reliable chain of narrators. Such authentic reports are found in the *Ṣaḥīḥ* of al-Bukhārī and similar sources. It is well established that ‘Alī had been gifted with an exceptional understanding in the Qur’ān.

There were some commentators who followed a pattern of transmitting the reports narrated from the early generation of Muslims (*salaf*) about the meaning of the Qur’ān. The first scholar who wrote something on that pattern is Mālik bin Anas.[1] Also included in this group of exegetes is al-Dāwūdī who was a student of al-Suyūṭī. ‘Iyāḍ has mentioned this briefly in *al-Madārik*.[2] The most famous among the followers of this pattern whose work is available to us is Muḥammad bin Jarīr al-Ṭabarī.

There were others who followed a pattern of reflection like Abū Isḥāq al-Zujāj and Abū ‘Alī al-Fārisī. Many others were engrossed in narrating the Isrā’īlī reports. As a result of that, fabricated reports were filled in their works. The process continued until there appeared in one age two great scholars, one in the east, namely ‘Allāmah Abū al-Qāsim Maḥmūd al-Zamakhsharī, the author of *al-Kashshāf*; and the other in the West, in Spain, namely al-Shaykh ‘Abd al-Ḥaqq bin ‘Aṭiyyah. The latter wrote his *tafsīr* under the title: *Al-Muḥarrir al-Wajīz*. Both of

1 Muḥammad bin ‘Alī bin Aḥmad al-Dāwūdī, *Ṭabaqāt al-Mufassirīn*, 2: 300.

2 ‘Iyāḍ bin Mūsā al-Yaḥṣubī, *Tartīb al-Madārik wa Taqrīb al-Masālik li Ma‘rifat Madhhabi Mālik*, Muḥammad Sālim Hāshim, ed. (Beirut: Dār al-Kutub al-‘Ilmiyyah, 1418/1998), 2: 93-94.

these works delve deep into the meaning of verses and marshal evidence from the Arabic language. These works also take notice of the discussions of other exegetes. One difference among the two is that in the work of al-Zamakhsharī, the aspects of Arabic language and its rhetoric are its focus, while in that of Ibn 'Aṭiyyah, the dimension of *sharī'ah* is more prominent. However, both works are pillars of this field and have been a great source for intelligent students after them.

The scholars of *tafsīr* had been in the habit of going deep in explaining the meaning of *ta'wīl* (hermeneutics) to show whether it was synonymous with *tafsīr* or more specific in relation thereto or different altogether. In short, there are some scholars who regard the two as equal. They include Tha'lab, Ibn al-A'rābī and Abū 'Ubaydah.[1] This also is apparently the view of al-Rāghib.[2] There are some other scholars who think that *tafsīr* relates to the manifest meaning, while *ta'wīl* is used for the metaphorical significations (*mutashābih*).[3] Still others say that *ta'wīl* means to transfer a word from its clear explicit meaning to another connotation supported by an argument.[4] Thus if the verse of the Qur'ān: "He causes the living to issue from the dead ..." is explained as: "causing the bird to issue from the egg ..." then it will be *tafsīr*. but if it is interpreted as "taking out the believer from the disbeliever" then this will be *ta'wīl*. There are other opinions with regard to the meaning of *tafsīr* and *ta'wīl*, but they are not worthy of notice. These are only terms over which no disputation is admissible. However, the linguistics and the reports support the first view; because *ta'wīl* is a verbal noun derived from *awwalahu*, which means to return something to its purported aim, and the purported aim of a word is its meaning and the connotation intended by the speaker, in this sense,

1 Muḥammad bin Mukram bin Manẓūr, *Lisān al-'Arab* (Qum: Nashr Adab al-Ḥawzah, 1405 AH), 5: 55, 11: 33-34.

2 Abū al-Qāsim al-Ḥusayn bin Muḥammad al-Rāghib al-Aṣfahānī, *al-Mufradāt fī Gharīb al-Qur'ān*, 380.

3 Muḥammad Murtaḍā al-Ḥusaynī al-Zabīdī, *Tāj al-'Urūs min Jawāhir al-Qāmūs*, Ḥusayn Naṣṣār, ed. (n.p.: Maṭba'at Ḥukūmat al-Kuwayt, 1394/1974), 11: 323-24.

4 Muḥammad bin Mukram bin Manẓūr, *Lisān al-'Arab*, 11: 33.

ta'wīl would be equivalent to *tafsīr*. However, the former is used only where the matter involves explaining a hidden but intelligible meaning.

The Qur'ān says: (7:53) "... Are they waiting for its (*ta'wīl*) fulfillment?" Here the word *ta'wīl* has been used in the sense of elaboration. And the Prophet (peace be upon him) in his prayer for Ibn 'Abbās said: "O Allah, grant him understanding in Religion and teach him explanation of meaning" *(ta'wīl)*.[1] Here the word *ta'wīl* means: "understanding the meaning of the Qur'ān".

In a tradition, 'Ā'ishah (may God be pleased with her) says: "The Prophet (peace be upon him) used to say in his *rukū'* (bowing in the prayers): *subhānak allāhumma Rabbanā wa bi ḥamdika, allāhumma ighfir lī*, and while so doing he was following the command of the Qur'ān."[2] What she meant was that he was following the command contained in the verse: "... celebrate the praises of your Lord and pray for His forgiveness": (110:3). That is why he combined in his prayer, *tasbīḥ* praise, mention of the word *Rabb* and asking forgiveness. Therefore, use of the word *ta'wīl* in this context by 'Ā'ishah (may God be pleased with her), clearly shows that the Prophet (peace be upon him) explained this verse by its explicit meaning and did not interpret it as an allusion to the end of his mission of Prophethood and imminence of his death, as understood from it by 'Umar and Ibn 'Abbās (may God be pleased with them).[3]

---

1 Aḥmad bin Muḥammad bin Ḥanbal, *al-Musnad*, Aḥmad Muḥammad Shākir, ed. (Cairo: Dār al-Ḥadīth, 1416/1995), 3: 95, ḥadīth no. 2397. The editor says about this ḥadīth, "Its *isnād* (chain) is authentic." See, ibid., footnote no. 2397.

2 Muḥammad bin Ismā'īl al-Bukhārī, *Ṣaḥīḥ al-Bukhārī* (Riyadh: Dār al-Salām, 1419/1999), 133, ḥadīth no. 817.

3 Muḥammad bin Jarīr al-Ṭabarī, *Jāmi' al-Bayān 'an Ta'wīl Āyy al-Qur'ān*, Aḥmad Abd al-Razzāq al-Bakrī, et al., eds. (Cairo: Dār al-Salām li al-Ṭibā'ah wa al-Nashr wa al-Tawzī' wa al-Tarjamah, 1429/2008), 10: 8816-17.

CHAPTER TWO

SOURCES OF THE SCIENCE OF TAFSĪR

In every science or discipline, there are certain prior sets of knowledge on which that science relies in the estimation of its founders. Through this *a priori* knowledge they establish the foundations of that science on a sound footing. In the classical terminology of Islamic sciences these sets of prior knowledge are named *istimdād* (sources of support). They are so named because that science needs their support to stand on a firm ground. This, however, does not mean that all contents of that science must depend on that set of supportive knowledge. It only means that that science stands on a firm ground on the basis of that supportive knowledge.

Further, whichever problems of other sciences happen to be discussed in a particular science are also not to be regarded as part of the supportive knowledge mentioned above. For example, the beneficial lengthy discussions of Fakhr al-Dīn al-Rāzī are not considered to be part of the supportive knowledge, nor could they be defined or delimited. The amount of such discussions depends on the measure of detail and proneness to excursus with the individual doctors of *tafsīr*.

The main substance of the supportive knowledge employed by an Arab scholar of *tafsīr* or one who has been initiated into Arabic lore is as follows: (I) knowledge of Arabic; (II) history of Arabs; (III) Traditions; and (IV) [Islamic Jurisprudence] principles of *fiqh*. According to some scholars, these sources of substantive knowledge also include: (V) Scholastics *(kalām)* and (VI) *qirā'āt* (Recitals of the Qur'ān).[1]

---

1 Al-Ālūsī, Abū al-Faḍl Shihāb al-Dīn al-Sayyid Maḥmūd, *Rūḥ al-Ma'ānī fī Tafsīr al-Qur'ān al-'Aẓīm wa al-Sab' al-Mathānī*, henceforth, *Rūḥ al-Ma'ānī*, Muḥammad Aḥmad

As to the knowledge of Arabic, it involves an understanding of the linguistic and literary lore of the Arabs. This understanding may either be acquired naturally, in the way the early Arabs among whom the Qur'ān was revealed had a natural gift for it. Or it could be acquired by learning, as was done by those who were later initiated into this tradition. They had interacted with the original Arabs and through long practice had obtained this understanding. There were some others who came later and studied Arabic linguistics and established its foundations as a distinct discipline.

Since the Qur'ān is in the Arabic language, the rules of Arabic grammar provide the means for its understanding. Without them, those who lack a natural gift for this language could fall prey to error and misunderstanding. By the rules of Arabic grammar, we mean the text of language, etymology, morphology, syntax, rhetoric and stylistics. In addition to this, it includes the consistent usage of the Arabs as reflected in the style and diction of their orations, poetics and the constructions employed by their prominent representatives of eloquence. Included in this are the prevailing familiar explanations by the original Arabs of Qur'ānic verses whose signification is not clear to later audiences.

The author of *al-Kashshāf* says: "it is the obligation of every exegete of the over-powering Book of Allah and His inimitable parole to maintain the Qur'ānic symmetry and rhetoric in their perfection; it is a perfection that challenged humanity to emulate it and remained free from any flaw that could undermine its inimitability. But if an exegete is unable to observe the primary requirements of linguistics in his task, then obviously he will remain short of his obligations to maintain the standards of symmetry and rhetoric."[1]

The fields of rhetoric and stylistics have a close nexus with the science of the exegesis if only because these are the means for

---

al-Amad and 'Umar 'Abd al-Salām al-Salāmī, eds. (Beirut: Dār Iḥyā' al-Turāth al-'Arabī and Mu'assasah al-Ta'rīkh al-'Arabī, 1420/1999), 1: 10.

1 Maḥmūd bin 'Umar al-Zamakhsharī, *al-Kashshāf*, 1: 186.

bringing out the features of Qur'ānic eloquence and communication and for showing the details of these features in the verses of the Qur'ān. It is these features that make the Qur'ān inimitable. That is why in the past, these fields of study (rhetoric and stylistics) were given the name of "arguments for the miraculousness of the Qur'ān" *(dalā'il al-i'jāz)*. The author of *al-Kashshāf* says: "The science of *tafsīr* is such a formidable field that every knowledgeable person cannot deal with it perceptively. For example, a jurist, even if he excels his contemporaries in the knowledge of legal edicts and injunctions, a theologian, even if he beats the whole world in the expertise of scholastics, the memorizer of stories and anecdotes, even if his memory is sharper than Ibn al-Qirriyyah, a preacher even if he is greater in his art than Ḥasan al-Baṣarī, a grammarian even if he is a greater master of grammar than Sībawayh and a linguist even if he chews linguistic subtleties with the force of his jaws, none of these men could countenance the challenge of treading its paths nor could delve in any manner of depth in the profound knowledge of *tafsīr*. There is only one exception to this: one who has mastered the two fields namely, "stylistics and rhetoric".[1]

Al-Zamakhsharī further says while commenting on the verse of the Qur'ān: "... and the heavens will be rolled up in His right hand..." (39:67): "there are so many verses in the Revelation and sayings of the Prophet (peace be upon him) whose subtle significations have been missed, even distorted by baseless hermeneutics attempted by those who have no nexus whatsoever with this branch of knowledge (i.e. stylistics and rhetoric). These people are unable to make any head or tail of it."[2]

Further, al-Sakkākī says in his introduction to the third section of his work: *al-Miftāḥ*: "And in what we have explained above is a note of warning that he who wants to grasp the purport of the speech of the

---

1 Ibid., 1: 96.

2 Ibid., 5: 322.

All Wise and All Holy in its totality, is in dire need of these two fields of knowledge [i.e. rhetoric and stylistics]. Woe, total woe unto those who treat *tafsīr* and tread its path while they are pedestrians in these two fields of study."[1]

Al-Sayyid al-Jurjānī, in his commentary on the work of al-Sakkākī, says: "doubtlessly the features of the Qur'ānic symmetry are more overwhelming than any other features. Therefore, he who is not naturally gifted in the understanding of Arabic rhetoric, must rely on these two disciplines" (i.e. rhetoric and stylistics).[2]

Al-Sakkākī has really hit the point by mentioning the Divine Attribute: "All Wise" in the above statement.[3] Because the language employed by the "All Wise" contains lofty objectives and precious meanings. One cannot encompass the whole or even part of them without a thorough practice in the rules of rhetoric that have been laid down in detail.

Further, by using the word: *yunabbihu* (gives a warning), he alludes to the fact that one is obliged to know the rhetorical features of the Qur'ān, though sometimes this aspect might escape notice by some people. And in his use of the word *fa al-waylu kulla al-wayl* ... (woe, total woe ...), there is discouragement. Because one who does not know both these disciplines, if he takes up a commentary of the Qur'ān and tries to bring out its subtle meanings, such a one will often fall into errors. Even if he rarely remains immune from error, he would still be guilty of attempting a task without being qualified for it."[4]

And his words: "understanding the total purport of the All-Wise ..." show that the aim of an exegete should be to grasp the total purport of Allah in the Qur'ān. This total grasp either means maximum urge to

---

1 Yūsuf bin Abī Bakr Muḥammad bin 'Alī al-Sakkākī, *Miftāḥ al-'Ulūm*, Na'īm Zarūr, ed. (Beirut: Dār al-Kutub al-'Ilmiyyah, 1403/1983), 162.

2 Al-Sayyad al-Sharīf 'Alī bin Muḥammad bin 'Alī al-Jurjānī, *al-Miṣbāḥ fī Sharḥ al-Miftāḥ*, Yūksal Jalīk, ed. (unpublished Ph.D thesis, Marmara University, Turkey, 2009), 29.

3 Ibid.

4 Ibid.

understand and extract subtle points so that one is prone to finding out the utmost meaning intended by Allah, The Most Exalted; or it means reaching the rhetorical dimensions incorporated in the Qur'ān. This latter aim could be attained only by knowing the demand of the context through an intense pursuit of this context. However, it should be borne in mind that each of the above two aspects requires a focus on something that is infinite. Each one of them calls for the utmost effort and exertion to understand. People vary in their understanding according to the purity of latent genius and availability of abundant knowledge.

Abū al-Walīd bin Rushd, while replying to someone who asserted that in understanding the Qur'ān, one did not need knowledge of the language of the Arabs, said:

"Such a one is ignorant; he should rather refrain from attempting it and should repent. Because nothing pertaining to the Religion of Islam could be correctly known without recourse to the language of Arabs. Allah says: … (it has been revealed) "in the clear Arabic language"… If then somebody asserts otherwise, he does so due to some impurity in his faith in religion. Such a person deserves to be taken to task by the leader of the Muslims for this utterance, as he deems appropriate, for this indeed is a serious utterance."[1]

As to the purport of al-Sakkākī's saying that one ought to grasp total meaning intended by Allah, it covers all that the language contains of special nuances. For example, he who explains the words of Allah: "Thee alone we worship", "إياك نعبد" as merely: "we worship you", such a one could not grasp the total meaning because he failed to notice the purpose of bringing the object before the subject.

Al-Sakkākī further says at the end of his discussion on stylistics *(al-Bayān)*: "I am not aware in the field of *tafsīr*, after the knowledge of its principles, of anything more helpful for a person to know the purpose of Allah by His speech, than the fields of rhetoric and stylistics. Nothing

1 Abū al-Walīd Muḥammad bin Aḥmad, Ibn Rushd (the grandfather), *Masā'il Abī al-Walīd bin Rushd*, Muḥammad al-Ḥabīb al-Tajkānī (ed.) (Beirut: Dār al-Jīl, 1993), 446-7.

is more helpful than these two in dealing with the interpretation of its figurative verses and in recognizing its subtle points and deeper nuances. Nor any other source comes to one's aid in discovering the miraculous aspects of the Qur'ān. There are so many verses in the Qur'ān that could not receive proper treatment and lost their whole luster and splendor when these were subjected to treatment by those who were not initiated in this knowledge. They attempted to explain it in unacceptable ways and interpreted it in a manner far from the intention of its Author."[1]

Al-Shaykh 'Abd al-Qāhir al-Jurjānī says in *Dalā'il al-I'jāz* at the end of the section on "interpretive metaphor": "It has been a habit of those who attempt exegesis without required knowledge to wrongly assign a literal meaning to the words that have been designed as metaphors and illustrations. They thereby corrupt the meaning and eliminate the intent of speech. They deprive themselves and the audience of the Qur'ān from knowing the locus of rhetoric and sublimity. You should not be misled by their occasional reference to these aspects and their immersion in that discussion. Because therein you will only come across innovation in ignorance and distortion.".[2]

As to the usage of the Arabs (referred to above as prerequisite for scholarship in Exegesis) it means full conversance with their diction and style as reflected in their orations, poetics, proverbs, habitual phrases and dialogues. This conversance, once acquired, would bring to a newly initiated learner of Arab lore a taste akin to the naturally gifted linguistic talent of an original Arab. By taste *(dhawq)* we mean "An inner condition of the self whereby it comprehends the various features and dimensions of eloquent speech".[3] Our teacher al-Jidd al-Wazīr says: "This condition is attained through a constant and

---

1 Yūsuf bin Abī Bakr Muḥammad bin 'Alī al-Sakkākī, *Miftāḥ al-'Ulūm*, 421.

2 'Abd al-Qāhir al-Jurjānī, *Kitāb Dalā'il al-I'jāz fī 'Ilm al-Ma'ānī*, henceforth, *Dalā'il al-I'jāz*, Muḥammad 'Abduhū et al., eds. (n.p.: Dār al-Manār, 1367 AH), 236.

3 'Abd al-Ḥakīm al-Siyālkotī, *Ḥāshiyat al-Siyālkotī 'alā Kitāb al-Muṭawwal li al-Taftāzānī*, Muḥammad al-Sayyid 'Uthmān (ed.) (Beirut: Dār al-Kutub al-'Ilmiyyah, 2012), 1: 120. (Ed.)

reflective pursuit of the usage of eloquent men. As a result thereof, a non-Arab acquires, by pursuing the occasions of usage and reflecting upon those specimens of language whose perfection in eloquence is established, the height of eloquence himself. Hence a claim to have this taste cannot be accepted except from the select few. And, this taste could vary in weakness or strength in relation to the intensity or otherwise of this reflective pursuit."

The ultimate credit is due to Allah for his saying that a scholar's reflective pursuit should aim those specimens that are established as highest examples of rhetorical excellence like the *Seven Odes* (*Al-Mu'allaqāt*) *al-Ḥamāsah*, *Nahj al-Balāghah*, *Muqāmāt al-Ḥarīrī* and the *Rasā'il* ('Epistles') by Badī' al-Zamān. The author of *al-Miftāh* also stresses the fact that a newcomer in this field of study cannot initially take up the appreciation of literary works of excellence on the basis of his taste like those who have naturally grown with a gifted taste. For in the beginning, he is bound to follow the verdict of the experts if he is devoid of the requisite taste. Thereafter, he will also gradually develop his own taste.[1]

For this reason, in order to create or perfect his taste, every exegete must, on some occasions, cite evidence in favor of the meaning present in the verse from the Arabic poetry or from any other genre of Arabic language in order to attain fuller taste, particularly on occasions where the meaning of the verse is not manifest. This will also be necessary to convince the listener and the learner who could not yet attain a full taste.

And all this – as stated before – is something beyond the rules of Arabic grammar and the principles of rhetoric. It is through this skill that certain layers of meaning are discovered and one's soul becomes contented with their understanding. When two parallel possibilities of interpretation of the Qur'ān present themselves, it is this skill whereby one prefers one of the possibilities and leaves the other.

1 Yūsuf bin Abī Bakr Muḥammad bin 'Alī al-Sakkākī, *Miftāḥ al-'Ulūm*, 169.

So we see that if someone attempts to interpret the verse:

> "O ye who believe, let not some men among you laugh at others: it may be that the latter are better than the former, nor let some women laugh at others ..." (49:11)

and he is faced with two possibilities whether:

(i) the conjunction between the word: *wa lā nisā'un* and *qawm* is one between exclusives *('atf mubāyin)*; (ii) this is one between the general and the particular. Then the commentator turned for illustration to the following line from Zuhayr:

> "I do not know, but hope to know; whether Āl Ḥiṣn were people or women."[1]

How could he be contented that this was a conjunction between exclusives rather than one between general and particular. This is supported by the following statement attributed to 'Abd Allāh bin 'Abbās:

"Poetry is the index of Arabs. When any word revealed by Allah in their language lacks clarity for us, we turn to this index and seek its comprehension therefrom."[2]

Ibn 'Abbās himself often cited Arabic poetry when asked about some words in the Qur'ān.[3]

Al-Qurṭubī reports the following: 'Ibn 'Abbās was asked about the meaning of the word *sinah* in the verse:

"no slumber can seize him nor sleep" (2:255) he answered: "that is slumber *(nu'ās)*." Then he cited this line of Zuhayr:[4]

"He is neither seized by slumber the whole night;

Nor does he sleep, nor is there any lie in his affairs."

---

1 Zuhayr bin Abī Salmā, *Dīwān Zuhayr bin Abī Salmā*, 'Alī Ḥasan Fā'ūr, ed. (Beirut: Dār al-Kutub al-'Ilmiyyah, 1408/1988), 17.

2 Jalāl al-Dīn 'Abd al-Raḥmān al-Suyūṭī, *al-Itqān,* 1: 382.

3 Ibid.

4 Muḥammad bin Aḥmad al-Qurṭubī, *al-Jāmi' li Aḥkām al-Qur'ān*, vol. 1, part 1, p. 33.

The Arab usage includes what is transmitted from the early elders *(salaf)* about their understanding of the meanings of some verses according to the rules of usage prevalent among them. For example, Imām Mālik has related in his *al-Muwaṭṭa'* on the authority of 'Urwah bin al-Zubayr, who says: "I asked 'Ā'ishah (may God be pleased with her) – and I was then young: 'Do you think that the words of Allah: "Behold: Ṣafā and Marwah are among the symbols of Allah, so if those who visit the House in the Season (of *Ḥajj*) or at other times (for *'Umrah*) should compass them round. It is no sin in them" (2:158) imply that if someone does not compass them round, then there is no blame on him?' 'Ā'ishah (may God be pleased with her) replied: 'By no means! If it were as you say, then it would have been: "There is no blame on them if they *do not* compass them round…".'"[1] Thus in this example, 'Ā'ishah (may God be pleased with her) explained the manner of Arabs' usage.

As to the reports transmitted in this connection, these pertain to the meaning of some verses that have come down to us from the Prophet (peace be upon him). These reports generally explain the occasions of difficulty or brevity in the Qur'ān. The quantum of these reports is not quite big. Ibn 'Aṭiyyah reports from 'Ā'ishah (may God be pleased with her) who says: "The Prophet (peace be upon him) did not explain except certain verses from the Qur'ān that were taught to him by Jibrīl."[2] Explaining this statement of 'Ā'ishah (may God be pleased with her), Ibn 'Aṭiyyah says: "It means those verses that pertained to the unseen matters or those verses that called for explication on account of their brevity. These are the verses whose explanation depends on an infallible source."[3] These reports include the statements of the

---

1 Mālik bin Anas, *al-Muwaṭṭa'*, Muḥammad Fu'ād 'Abd al-Bāqī, ed. (Beirut: Dār Iḥyā' al-Turāth al-'Arabī, n.d.), 1: 273.

2 'Abd al-Ḥaqq bin Ghālib bin 'Aṭiyyah al-Andalusī, *al-Muḥarrir al-Wajīz fī Tafsīr al-Kitāb al-'Azīz*, henceforth, *al-Muḥarrir al-Wajīz*, 'Abd Allāh bin Ibrāhīm al-Anṣārī and 'Abd al-'Āl al-Sayyid Ibrāhīm, eds., 2nd ed. (n.p.: n.p., n.d.), 1: 28.

3 Ibid.

Companions who witnessed the revelation, such as the particular circumstances attending certain revelations *(asbāb al-nuzūl)*, the abrogating and the abrogated verses, explanation of some ambiguity, or elaboration of a certain event that might be relevant to a particular revelation. However, in all the above matters, the Companions relied on the reports transmitted on the authority of the Prophet (peace be upon him) rather than their own opinions. For example, explaining the meaning of: "those who incurred wrath" (1:7) as referring to the Jews. In the same way, on the basis of these reports, the meaning of the verse: "leave me alone to deal with the one whom I created alone …" (74:11) was thought to refer to al-Walīd bin al-Mughīrah al-Makhzūmī, father of Khālid bin al-Walīd (may God be pleased with him), and that of the verse: "have you seen the one who rejects our signs, yet says: I shall certainly be given wealth and children?" (19:77) to point to al-'Āṣ bin Wā'il al-Sahmī in his dispute with Khabbāb bin al-Arat as reported in *Ṣaḥīḥ al-Bukhārī* in the commentary on the chapter Maryam.[1] Ibn 'Abbās says that for one year he wanted to ask 'Umar (may God be pleased with him) about the ladies who had backed each other up against the Prophet (peace be upon him), but only his awe prevented him from that. Eventually he did ask him. "They are 'Ā'ishah and Ḥafṣah", replied 'Umar (may God be pleased with him).[2]

But when we say that the account of the occasions and circumstances of the revelation are part of the *tafsīr* material, it only means that these accounts help explain the purport of the Qur'ān. These accounts by no means limit the text of a verse to a particular circumstance or occasion, because the occasions of the revelation do not qualify the text of the Qur'ān.

Taqiyy al-Dīn al-Subkī says: Just as any occasion of the revelation *(sabab al-nuzūl)* does not qualify, so the particular aim of an expression does not qualify. For example, if a particular matter is mentioned and

1 Muḥammad bin Ismā'īl al-Bukhārī, *Ṣaḥīḥ al-Bukhārī*, 823, ḥadīth no. 4732.

2 Ibid., 873-74, ḥadīth no. 4913-15.

then it is followed by a general direction, the mention of the former shall not serve as a qualifier. An example of this principle is the verse: "... so there is no blame on them if they arrange an amicable settlement between themselves; and such settlement is best" (4:128).[1]

At times, a report about the occasion of the revelation is helpful in elaborating and interpreting an apparent connotation which is not intended by that verse. An example of this case is the reliance by Qudāmah bin Maẓ'ūn (may God be pleased with him) on the verse: "on those who believe and do the righteous deeds, there is no blame for what they ate" (5:93) in his defense before 'Umar bin al-Khaṭṭāb (may God be pleased with him) for drinking an intoxicant. Qudāmah was appointed Governor of Baḥrayn by 'Umar (may God be pleased with him). The Governor was accused of drinking. When 'Umar (may God be pleased with him) confronted him with the evidence in order to enforce punishment of lashing on him for his offense, he pleaded defense on the basis of the above verse. But 'Umar (may God be pleased with him) rejected his plea on the grounds of his wrong interpretation of this verse and its misapplication by him to his own case. On the request of the Khalīfah, Ibn 'Abbās presented before him the correct interpretation of the verse, which according to a report from the Prophet (peace be upon him), applied exclusively to those believers who drank before the express prohibition of intoxicants. Therefore, 'Umar (may God be pleased with him) confirmed the interpretation put forward by Ibn 'Abbās.[2] These reports (about the meaning of certain verses of the Qur'ān) also include the consensus of the Muslim community on the interpretation of some verses. This is because such a consensus could not be without reliance on an authoritative report. For example, there is a consensus concerning the

1 Taqī al-Dīn al-Subkī, *Fatāwā al-Subkī* (Beirut: Dār al-Ma'ārif, n.d.), 1: 43-45.

2 Muḥammad bin 'Abd Allāh al-Ḥākim, *al-Mustadrak 'alā al-Ṣaḥīḥayn*, Maḥmūd Maṭrajī, ed. (Beirut: Dār al-Fikr, 1421/2001), 5: 293; 'Abd al-Razzāq bin Hammām al-Ṣan'ānī, *al-Muṣannaf*, Ḥabīb al-Raḥmān al-A'ẓamī ed. (Johannesburg: Majlis Ilmi, 1392/1972), 9: 240-43.

first verse relating to those who leave no descendants or ascendants (*kalālah* mentioned in 4:12) that the 'sister' mentioned in it means a sister from the mother's side.[1] Similarly, there is a consensus among the Muslim scholars that the 'prayer' mentioned in 62:9-10, means the Friday prayer.[2] Likewise, there is an established consensus of the community on all the essentials of Islam such as the meaning of words; that *ṣalāt* it is constituted by a particular mode of worship and that *zakāt* is a peculiar form of paid wealth.

As to the variant readings of the Qur'ān, these are needed only when an argument is sought from a reading in favor of a different explanation. This recourse to a different reading serves the purpose of finding a reason for preferring one of the meanings established by a verse or to further elaborate a meaning. In such a case, the reading is cited in the manner of providing an illustration from the Arabic language. Because if that reading is well-known, then it must be regarded as strong linguistic evidence. And if that reading is rare, then its value shall not lie in its being a report *(riwāyah)* because it will not be an authentic report on account of its rarity. Its value will lie in the fact that its reciter has recited it according to the correct Arabic usage. Because no reciter is worthy of consideration unless the soundness of his Arabic knowledge has been well-known. I have also included the annals of Arabs in the required sources of *tafsīr* because these are part of their general literature and I have done that to dispel doubts in some minds about their futility, because recourse to these annals helps in comprehending what is mentioned in the Qur'ān briefly. Indeed the Qur'ān mentions stories and anecdotes for the purpose of their moral lessons and certainly not for the sake of entertainment. Through recourse to this record of Arab history, many subtle meanings of verses could be comprehended.

---

1 Muḥammad bin Aḥmad al-Qurṭubī, *al-Jāmi' li Aḥkām al-Qur'ān*, 3: 1: 69.

2 Abū Ḥafṣ 'Umar bin 'Alī bin 'Ādil al-Ḥanbalī, *al-Lubāb fī 'Ulūm al-Kitāb*, 'Ādil Ahmad 'Ābd al-Mawjūd et al., eds. (Beirut: Dār al-Kutub al-'Ilmiyyah, 1419/1998), 19: 84.

For example, the meaning of the following verses:

(1) "And be not like her who undoes the thread which she has spun after it has become strong" (16:92); and

(2) "Cursed were the people of the Ditch..." (in the story of the boy and the king) (85:4).

depends on finding out the stories of people referred to in these verses, from the sources of Arab history.

As to the principles of jurisprudence (*uṣūl al-fiqh*) these have not been included by the scholars in the *tafsīr* material. However, they do mention in their discussions the general rules of commands and prohibitions that are part of the *uṣūl al-fiqh*. It thus appears that some of these things do form part of the *tafsīr* material, especially from the following two ways:

(i) where the science of *uṣūl* contains issues relating to the modes of Arabic usage and the linguistic problems neglected by the scholars of Arabic language like the issues pertaining to inner or implied meaning *(faḥwā)*[1] and the opposite implication *(mafhūm al-mukhālafah)*. Imām Ghazālī has also counted the science of *uṣūl* among those sciences that are related to the Qur'ān and its commandments.[2] Therefore, this science must form part of the material on *tafsīr*;

---

1 *Faḥwā* in the usage of Arabs and Qur'ānic Sciences pertains to several related ideas which can be summarized as follows:

i- That which is implied by a word or statement but not from its literal sense. For instance the Qur'ān says: "Say not to them "Uff!" nor chide them, but speak unto them a noble word." Although the verse literally prohibits rebuking parents, by implication, it also prohibits beating them. (Abū Hilāl al-'Askarī);

ii- Using a clear word to imply a hidden or implicit meaning (Ibn al-Qayyim al-Jawziyyah);

iii- Mentioning 'few' but implying 'many' and mentioning 'many' but implying 'few'. (al-Zarkashī). [Ed.]

2 Muḥammad bin Muḥammad al-Ghazālī, *Iḥyā' 'Ulūm al-Dīn* (n.p.: Maktabah wa Maṭba'ah Karyāṭah Fūtarā, n.d.), 1: 18.

(ii) since the science of *uṣūl* regulates the rules of deduction and elaborates them, it serves as an instrument for the exegete to derive the purposes of the *sharī'ah* from its verses.

Also, 'Abd al-Ḥakīm Siyālkōtī and al-Ālūsī have adopted the opinion of al-Sakkākī in regarding *'ilm al-kalām* as one of the necessary sources of the science of *tafsīr*. This, according to Siyālkōtī, is because this science depends on establishing the factum that God is the Speaker. Therefore, it stands in need of *'ilm al-kalām.*[1]

Al-Ālūsī adds: "... this is due to the necessity of understanding what sort of speech was appropriate for God and what was impossible for Him."[2] He was referring to the figurative verses relating to Divine Attributes like "The Most Gracious rose over the Throne" (20:5).

This explanation is akin to that of Siyālkōtī, mentioned above. However, both are confusing. Because the Qur'ān's being a Divine speech had been well-established among the early elders *(salaf)* even before the emergence of the science of scholastics *('ilm al-kalām)*, it therefore had no bearing on *tafsīr* as such. As to the knowledge about appropriate and impossible speech, this knowledge also preceded *tafsīr*. However, the need to include the science of scholastics in *tafsīr* may arise when an elaborate discussion is made about the impossibility of certain connotations of Qur'ānic verses. And I have already explained that the material drawn by an elaborate discussant in the Qur'ān does not make that material part of the substantive subject matter of the Qur'ān.

Unlike al-Suyūṭī,[3] we have not included *fiqh* in the *tafsīr* material because understanding of the Qur'ān does not depend on the issues of *fiqh*. The latter is subsequent to the former and has issued from it as its branch. An exegete needs to agitate the issues of *fiqh* only when he

1 'Abd al-Ḥakīm al-Siyālkōtī, *Ḥāshiyat al-'Allāmah 'Abd al-Ḥakīm al-Siyālkōtī 'alā al-Tafsīr li al-Qāḍī al-Bayḍāwī* (Quetta: Maktabah Islāmiyyah, n.d.), 13.

2 Al-Ālūsī, Abū al-Faḍl Shihāb al-Dīn al-Sayyid Maḥmūd, *Rūḥ al-Ma'ānī*, 1: 10.

3 Jalāl al-Dīn 'Abd al-Raḥmān al-Suyūṭī, *al-Itqān*, 2: 1211.

intends to undertake a detailed discussion of these issues in his work. He then needs to go into the details of the modes of deduction in order to elaborate the meanings of verses having legal, cultural and intellectual import. Therefore, it is almost impossible to count accurately all those sources of knowledge that an elaborate discussant of the Qur'ān might depend upon. For such a one is quite likely to require all the (Islamic) sciences. It was to this latter fact that al-Bayḍāwī was referring when he said "It does not behove someone to deal with *tafsīr* and to take up the challenge of participating in this formidable field unless he has an in-depth knowledge in all the religious sciences, both in their roots and in their branches as well as in all the categories of Arabic linguistics and genres of literature."[1]

It should be borne in mind that the reports transmitted from the Prophet (peace be upon him) about the meanings of verses are not considered among the auxiliaries of *tafsīr* because these constitute the very substance of *tafsīr*. Nor should those verses of the Qur'ān that explain, limit, qualify, elaborate, interpret or throw light on other verses be included in the auxiliary sources of *tafsīr*, for the same reason. It should also be borne in mind that, notwithstanding the borrowing made in *tafsīr* from the above sources of knowledge, the former occupies the top position in all Islamic sciences. Whatever is borrowed in its discussions from other sources is only meant to elaborate its concise contents so that all aspects and dimensions of its latent significations are laid bare.

---

1 'Abd Allāh bin 'Umar bin Muḥammad al-Shīrāzī al-Bayḍāwī, *Anwār al-Tanzīl*, 2.

CHAPTER THREE

ON THE AUTHENTICITY OF *TAFSĪR* WITHOUT RELIANCE ON TRANSMITTED REPORTS AND THE MEANING OF *TAFSĪR* BASED ON OPINION

It might be said that the sources of knowledge we have identified as essential for *tafsīr* show that a great deal of commentary on the Qur'ān is possible without reliance on the relevant reports transmitted from the Prophet (peace be upon him) or his Companions. That any person, you might say, who is fully equipped with these sources could easily discover the meaning of the Qur'ān and interpret its verses by his own predilection even though it might not be attributed to these authoritative reports. If this is the case, then what is the status of the warning given in the tradition related by al-Tirmidhī on the authority of Ibn 'Abbās that the Prophet (peace be upon him) said: "He who opines on the Qur'ān by his own judgment should occupy his position in the Hell"?[1] And what will you do with other similar reports that strike a note of caution against speaking about the Qur'ān without knowledge? And, further, how would you then explain the extreme self-restraint exercised by some of the early scholars in the sphere of *tafsīr* without any authoritative reports? Besides, we have the following reply of Abū Bakr al-Ṣiddīq (may God be pleased with him) when he was asked to explain the meaning of the word "*abb*" occurring in the verse (80:31) "… and fruits and fodder …", he said: "What earth will carry me and which sky shall cover me if I opined in the Qur'ān by my own judgment?"[2] There

1 Muḥammad bin 'Īsā al-Tirmidhī, *Jāmi' al-Tirmidhī* (Riyadh: Dār al-Salām, 1420/1999), 663, ḥadīth no. 2951. Al-Tirmidhī comments on this ḥadīth: "This ḥadīth is *ḥasan*".

2 'Abd Allāh bin Muḥammad bin Abī Shaybah, *al-Muṣannaf*, Muḥammad 'Awwāmah, ed. (Beirut: Dār Qurtabah li al-Tibā'at wa al-Nashr wa al-Tawzī', 1427/2006), 15: 500, ḥadīth no. 30731.

are similar reports about Sa'īd bin al-Musayyib and al-Sha'bī to the effect that they refrained from this practice.[1]

As you might well have supposed, I find myself affirming this position and considering it tenable. This is because expansion in *tafsīr* and intellectual development toward deriving meanings from the Qur'ān has been possible due to those who were given the gift of understanding in the Book of Allah. Is it possible to reach a concrete realization of the famous dictum about the Qur'ān that it is a book "whose wonders are endless"[2] without elaborating its meanings through expansion in *tafsīr*? If there were no such expansion, the work of *tafsīr* would have remained confined to a few pages. And we have the following statement of 'Ā'ishah (may God be pleased with her): "the Prophet of Allah (peace be upon him) did not interpret the Qur'ān except for a few verses that were taught to him by Jibrīl",[3] to bear us out.

Further, if *tafsīr* were confined to assigning linguistic meanings of individual words, then this material would have been scanty. Also we find an abundance of opinions of the early elders from amongst the Companions and those immediately after them about the explication of Qur'ānic verses. And a great number of these opinions are based on their own knowledge and understanding that they applied in deducing the meaning of the Qur'ān. In this respect, al-Ghazālī[4] and al-Qurṭubī[5] say the following:

"It is not correct to suppose that whatever has been said by the Companions about *tafsīr* was heard by them from the Prophet (peace be upon him) for two reasons:

---

1 Ibid., 15: 498, ḥadīth no. 30724; Muḥammad 'Abd al-'Aẓīm al-Zarqānī, *Manāhil al-'Irfān fī 'Ulūm al-Qur'ān* (Beirut: Dār al-Fikr, 1424/2004), 2: 42.

2 Muḥammad bin 'Īsā al-Tirmidhī, *Jāmi' al-Tirmidhī*, 653, ḥadīth no. 2906. Al-Tirmidhī comments on this ḥadīth: "This is a *gharīb* ḥadīth … and its chain (*isnād*) is unknown (*majhūl*).

3 'Abd al-Ḥaqq bin Ghālib bin 'Aṭiyyah al-Andalusī, *al-Muḥarrir al-Wajīz*, 1: 28.

4 Muḥammad bin Muḥammad al-Ghazālī, *Iḥyā' 'Ulūm al-Dīn*, 1: 291.

5 Muḥammad bin Aḥmad al-Qurṭubī, *al-Jāmi' li Aḥkām al-Qur'ān*, 1: 1: 39.

(i) explanation of only a small number of verses has been established from the Prophet (peace be upon him), as proved in the above cited statement of 'Ā'ishah (may God be pleased with her);

(ii) the Companions have also varied in their views on *tafsīr* in different ways and it is not possible to reconcile these differing views". Hence it is impossible to assume that all these differing views might have come down from the Prophet (peace be upon him). And if some of these views were indeed heard from the Prophet (peace be upon him), then other differing views should have been abandoned. This means that if some of them were really based on statements of the Prophet (peace be upon him), then its exponents would have made this fact known. And had they revealed their source, then surely others who differed with them would have left their own opinions and would have adopted the former. Thus it is established that everyone who explained a verse of the Qur'ān did so on the basis of what became evident to him by his own deduction. Al-Bukhārī relates in his *Ṣaḥīḥ* on the authority of Abū Juḥayfah who says: 'I asked 'Alī: "do you have any knowledge of the Revelation beside what is in the Book of Allah? 'Alī said: "by the One who splits the seed-grain and creates man, I know nothing save that understanding which Allah gives someone about the Qur'ān."[1] Also, it is reported that the Prophet of Allah (peace be upon him) made the following prayer for 'Abd Allāh bin 'Abbās: "O Allāh, grant him understanding in Religion and teach him interpretation".[2] The scholars are agreed that the word *ta'wīl* occurring in this prayer means *ta'wīl* al-Qur'ān.

1 Muḥammad bin Ismā'īl al-Bukhārī, *Ṣaḥīḥ al-Bukhārī*, 504, ḥadīth no. 3047.

2 Aḥmad bin Muḥammad bin Ḥanbal, *al-Musnad*, 3: 95, ḥadīth no. 2397. The editor says about this ḥadīth, "Its *isnād* (chain) is authentic." See, ibid., footnote no. 2397.

Our jurists have said in their discussion of the etiquette of reciting the Qur'ān that comprehending the meaning of the Qur'ān, even little recitation, was better than reciting it without comprehension. This is what Imām al-Ghazālī says in *Iḥyā'*:

"Reflective reading of the Qur'ān means revisiting its meaning again and again. And understanding means discovering the most apt meaning of each verse in order to arrive at those deeper meanings that reveal themselves to the few fortunate ones."[1]

Al-Ghazālī goes on to say: "among the impediments to one's understanding is to suppose that only whatever has been transmitted from Ibn 'Abbās and Mujāhid in a *tafsīr*, supplied the meaning of the Qur'ān and the rest is only a *tafsīr* based on individual views. This kind of thinking is a great hindrance in one's understanding of the Qur'ān."[2]

Imām Rāzī had the following to say while explaining the verse of the Qur'ān: "And live with them in accordance with virtuous ways[3] ... it has been established in the principles of jurisprudence that if the early scholars mention one aspect in explaining a verse, then this is no bar to the later scholars' discovering some other aspect of it. For otherwise all those subtle meanings discovered by the later scholars shall be liable to rejection. And such a view could only be held by a retrogressive imitator."[4]

Sufyān bin 'Uyaynah once said while commenting on the verse: "never think Allah negligent of what the wrong-doers do" (14:42): "it is a consolation for the victim and a warning for the wrong doer." When he was asked about the source of this explanation, he was annoyed and said: "this has been said by one who knows the meaning

---

1 Muḥammad bin Muḥammad al-Ghazālī, *Iḥyā' 'Ulūm al-Dīn*, 1: 283-84.

2 Muḥammad bin Muḥammad al-Ghazālī, *Iḥyā' 'Ulūm al-Dīn*, 1: 286.

3 Imām Rāzī mentions the following text while commenting on 4:3, not on 4:19 as Ibn 'Āshūr thinks.

4 Al-Fakhr al-Rāzī, *al-Tafsīr al-Kabīr* (Cairo: Mu'assasat al-Maṭbū'āt al-Islāmiyyah, n.d.), 9: 170.

himself."[1] And Abū Bakr bin al-'Arabī says in *Al-'Awāṣim* that he had dictated five hundred issues on the chapter Nūḥ and eight hundred on the story of Prophet Mūsa (AS) in the Qur'ān.[2]

Is the nature of legislative injunctions deduced from the Qur'ān during the first three centuries of Islam in any way different from explaining the verses in an unprecedented way? We find Imām al-Shāfi'ī saying: "I searched for an argument in favor of consensus as a binding source of law until I found it in the verse:

'if anyone contends with the Messenger even after Guidance has been plainly conveyed to him and follows a path other than that becoming to men of faith, we shall leave him in the path he has chosen and land him in Hell; what an evil refuge! (4:115)'."[3]

In his commentary on *al-Khashshāf*, Sharaf al-Dīn al-Ṭībī says while talking about the chapter "Poets": "the condition for a correct *tafsīr* is that it is in accordance with the prevalent usage of the word, free from artificiality and forced meaning."[4] The author of *al-Khashshāf* considers all other kinds of *tafsīr* as heretical.[5]

Doubt created by the reports that contain warning against attempting *tafsīr* by individual opinion may be explained in the following five ways:

i) here individual opinion means saying something that occurs to one's mind without any reflective pursuit of the arguments relating to linguistics, the objectives of the *sharī'ah* and its variables, necessary knowledge about the

---

1 Maḥmūd bin 'Umar al-Zamakhsharī, *al-Kashshāf*, 3: 389.

2 Al-Qāḍī Abū Bakr Muḥammad bin 'Abd Allāh bin al-'Arabī, *Kitāb al-'Awāsim min al-Qawāṣim*, 'Abd al-Ḥamīd bin Bādīs, ed. (n.p.: al-Maṭba'ah al-Jazā'iriyyah al-Islāmiyyah, 1345/1926). Unfortunately, we couldn't locate the source for this narration. (Ed.)

3 'Abd al-Malik bin 'Abd Allāh bin Yūsuf al-Juwaynī, *al-Burhān fī Uṣūl al-Fiqh*, 'Abd al-'Aẓīm al-Dīb, ed. (Doha: Maṭābi' al-Dawḥah al-Ḥadīthah, 1399 AH), 1: 677.

4 Sharaf al-Dīn al-Ḥusayn bin 'Abd Allāh al-Ṭībī, *Futūḥ al-Ghayb 'an Kashf Qinā' al-Rayb* [from *Sūrat al-Anbiyā'* to *Sūrat al-Shu'arā'*], 'Abd al-Quddūs Rājī Muḥammad Mūsā, ed. (MA Thesis, al-Jāmi'at al-Islāmiyyah, al-Madīnat al-Munawwarah, 1416 AH), 576.

5 Maḥmūd bin 'Umar al-Zamakhsharī, *al-Kashshāf*, 4: 400.

abrogating and the abrogated verses and their injunctions, and the occasions of the Revelation; such an attempt, no doubt, is bound to meet with failure even if per chance the conclusion is correct.

Because it will still be an attempt to conceptualize the meaning without proper knowledge; such an attempt is devoid of guarantees of authenticity. It will be like "many a (hitting) shot is there without a (skilled) shooter", as the saying goes.[1] This kind of attempt at *tafsīr* will be similar to the one who had explained *Alif Lām Mīm* as: "Allāh sent down Jibrīl with the Qur'ān to Muḥammad"; obviously such attempts have no ground to stand on.

As to the reluctance of Abū Bakr al-Ṣiddīq to explain a certain verse as reported above, this was due to sheer piety and an utter apprehension of falling into error in respect of those things in which he did not find a sound argument or where there was no need to attempt any *tafsīr*. When he was asked about the meaning of *kalālah* in the last verse of the chapter "The Women" he said: "I will express my view; if it is correct, then it will be from God, and if wrong, then it will be from me and the devil."[2]

The same explanation applies to reports that al-Sha'bī and Sa'īd kept themselves away from any attempt that involved even a remote possibility for error. All this was an expression of extreme piety on their part. For, otherwise, God has charged us in such matters with the duty of exhausting effort based on the hope of reaching probable correctness of conclusion.

---

1 The saying is *rubba ramyatin min ghayr rāmin* although the author mentions *ramyatun min ghayr rāmin*. This would be translated as "Many a (hitting) shot is there without a (skilled) shooter". [Ed.]

2 'Abd al-Raḥmān bin Abī Bakr al-Suyūṭī, *al-Durr al-Manthūr fī al-Tafsīr bi al-Ma'thūr* (Beirut: Dār al-Kutub al-'Ilmiyyah, 1421/2000), 2: 443.

ii) when someone does not adequately reflect on the Qur'ān and explains it superficially without encompassing all the dimensions of the verse, confining himself to some of the arguments and leaving the rest, then he will come under the scope of this warning. For example, if he depends on one aspect of Arabic language to the exclusion of other aspects. An instance of such unacceptable *tafsīr* is to explain the verse (4:79): "whatever good falls to your lot is from God" on the basis of its apparent meaning and to say that "all good is from God and every evil is the handiwork of man" without considering the established doctrine of the *sharī'ah* that nothing happens without Divine Will. Such a person has ignored the foregoing verse: "say all is by God's Will" (4:78). Another instance of such a baseless *tafsīr* is to explain something merely on the basis of what appears to be a simple sense of a word in the Arabic language without finding out the wider usage of that word. An instance of such a mistaken *tafsīr* is to explain the verse: "and we sent to the Thamūd a she-camel as a visible sign." (17:59), as a "seeing she-camel that is not blind". Such an attempt is an example of explaining the Qur'ān by one's opinion which has been condemned due to its mischievous nature.

iii) when someone is biased or tilted to any particular school or sect and he forces an interpretation on the Qur'ān according to his preferred view, thereby deviating from the purport of the Qur'ān and its well-known meaning. He drags evidence from the Qur'ān to support his own point of view. The intelligence of such a biased man is straitjacketed by his prior prejudice. Apart from his own school's point of view, nothing otherwise occurs to his mind. Even if any flash of truth shines before him and a meaning different from his school's view appears to him, he is overpowered by the devil of prejudice who dissuades him from that suggestion. For example someone takes *Istiwā' 'ala al-'arsh* (occurring in 20:5) to mean occupying or settling on it. If it occurred to him that the meaning of the Divine attribute *Al-Quddūs* is that Allah is purified of all attributes of the created ones, his rigid attachment to his own school will deter that meaning to settle in his mind. Even if that meaning persists in his thinking, his intellect will travel on to discover a second or third meaning. He will turn back every notion contrary to his own school. Because rigid adherence to a superficial sense of the word prevents him from delving into deeper meanings.

Another example of this deviation is the interpretation put forward by the Mu'tazilah for the verse: "and some faces that day shall be shining and radiant looking at their Lord" (75:22-23) to mean that "they shall be *waiting* for the bounty of their Lord". Here they have suggested that the word *ilā* (a preposition) is a singular of *ālā'*, meaning bounties.[1] This despite the fact that it is contrary to the explicit connotation, transmitted meaning and the whole purport of this verse.

iv) to explain the Qur'ān on the basis of an opinion formed by a verbal connotation and then insisting that this was precisely the intended meaning of the Qur'ān to the exclusion of any other. The purpose of this rigid constriction is to leave no room for others to interpret the Qur'ān in a broader perspective;

v) the warning given in some reports is meant to stress extreme caution and care in reflecting upon the Qur'ān and interpreting it to avoid jumping to conclusions. In this respect Muslim scholars have shown varying levels of restraint. Some of them exercised an excessive degree of caution, to the extent of restraining themselves from explaining anything in the Qur'ān without referring to an authentic source. The famous

1 Muḥammad bin Aḥmad al-Qurṭubī, *al-Jāmi' li Aḥkām al-Qur'ān*, vol. 10, part 1, p. 99.

> master of linguistics and literature al-Aṣmaʻī never attempted to explain any word of Arabic if it was a word occurring in the Qur'ān.[1]

This is the kind of apprehension that dominates some people, particularly men of exceptional knowledge and talents. Also in some states of mind they are dominated by such fears, while in others they are not. The truth of the matter is that, leaving aside issues involving the principles of belief, Allah has not made us responsible for anything beyond reaching a probable conclusion based on valid argument. And arguments vary according to the nature of the issue in question.

As to those who take a rigid stand that the explanation of the Qur'ān must not go beyond what has been reported *(ma'thūr)*, they have overstretched the meaning of this word (i.e. *ma'thūr*). Yet they could not clearly define their intended meaning from the use of this word. They could not explain from whom the reports ought to be transmitted. If by this they mean the reports from the Prophet (peace be upon him) concerning the explanation of some verses, transmitted through an authentic and acceptable chain of narrators, then they have narrowed down the vast expanse of the meanings of the Qur'ān. They have placed a bar on the fountains of wide categories of knowledge that are derived from the Qur'ān. At the same time, they contradicted their own stand in the works of *tafsīr* they compiled themselves, and refuted their own elders *(salaf)* in the interpretations they have put forward. Then they cannot escape the confession that the great scholars of Islam among the Companions and their successors did not confine themselves to relate the *tafsīr* that reached them from the Prophet (peace be upon him). 'Umar bin al-Khaṭṭāb used to ask scholars about the meaning of a great many verses. However, he never required them to relate only what had reached them from the Prophet (peace be upon him). And if by the transmitted report *(ma'thūr)* they mean what is related from the Prophet

1 Muḥammad bin Yazīd al-Mubarrid, *al-Kāmil*, Muḥammad Aḥmad al-Dālī, ed. (Beirut: Mu'assasat al-Risālah, 1406/1986), 3: 1435.

(peace be upon him) and the Companions only – as appears in the work by al-Suyūṭī *al-Durr al-Manthūr* – even then such a narrow scope will admit but little material and will not be sufficient to dispense with the scholars of *tafsīr*. Because whatever has been related from the majority of the Companions is scant material save that which is reported from 'Ālī bin Abī Ṭālib. Even the latter source contains both correct and weak – even fabricated – reports. Further, it has been correctly reported from him that he said: "I have no knowledge beside what is in the Book of Allah except an understanding that is granted by Allah."[1] Apart from these, there are reports transmitted from Ibn Masʿūd, 'Abd Allāh bin 'Umar, Anas and Abū Hurayra. As for Ibn 'Abbās, most of what has come down from him is in the nature of his own views reported in various ways by his narrators.

And if they mean by the transmitted reports *(ma'thūr)* whatever was narrated before the compilation of the earliest works on *tafsīr* like what has been related from the followers of Ibn 'Abbās and Ibn Masʿūd, then they have thereby opened the gate from one side and have drawn themselves nearer that opening. For they could not then escape admitting the fact that these successors of the Companions *(tābi'ūn)* have been saying many things about the Qur'ān on the basis of their own understanding of the Book. They neither claimed any authoritative source for their statements nor reported any deletion of the chain of reporters. And in respect of numerous verses, their opinions varied. This fact shows that these statements were based on their own understanding.

Those who are familiar with their views are quite aware of this fact. This fact is also established in the work on *tafsīr* by al-Ṭabarī and similar other works. Al-Ṭabarī in his work always confines himself to mention whatever has been related from the Companions and their successors. However, he does not stop there. He goes beyond that. He reflects and prefers some of the reported views over others on the basis of evidence cited by him from the usage of Arabs. Even this much

1 Muḥammad bin Ismā'īl al-Bukhārī, *Ṣaḥīḥ al-Bukhārī*, 1190, ḥadīth no. 6903.

liberty is enough to show that he did not remain confined to the transmitted reports *(ma'thūr)*. He was preceded in this respect by Baqiyy bin Makhlad whose work on *tafsīr* is not available to us.[1] Some of the contemporaries of Al-Ṭabarī also followed his way like Ibn Ḥātim, Ibn Mardwayh and al-Ḥākim. However, credit is due to those who did not imprison themselves in the *tafsīr* of the Qur'ān on the basis of the transmitted reports only, like al-Farrā' and Abū 'Ubaydah among the early commentators and al-Zujāj and al-Rummānī among the later ones. Their way was followed after them by al-Zamakhsharī and Ibn 'Aṭiyyah.

As we have cited above some examples of *tafsīr* on the basis of condemnable opinions, we will not pass without sounding caution against a group of people who follow their whims in the *tafsīr* of the Qur'ān. They have taken the words of the Qur'ān away from their manifest meanings which they call the "occult". These people suppose that the Qur'ān has been sent down containing figurations and symbols that represent certain aims. This group of people actually originated from *shī'ah* extremists known among the scholars as *Bāṭiniyyah*. They were so named by them because this was how they (the scholars) identified them. Among the historians they are called Ismā'īlis since they attributed their sect to Ja'far bin Ismā'īl al-Ṣādiq. The group believed in his infallibility and assumption of their leadership after his father, on the basis of his will in that regard. People of this group believe that it was essential for Muslims to have a "leader of guidance" from the family of the Prophet. Such a leader alone could establish religion and express the will of Allah. When these people felt that they will be disputed in their stance by the scholars on the basis of arguments from the Qur'ān and the *Sunnah*, they found no refuge against it except constructing their own hermeneutics to explain away the arguments that could challenge their heresy. However, they thought that if they applied their peculiar interpretation to those arguments only, they

1 There are reports that 11 volumes of Baqiyy bin Makhlad's *tafsīr* work have been found in a library in Turkey and a team of scholars has started work on it. (Ed).

would be accused of prejudice and arbitrary thinking. Therefore, they turned the whole Qur'ān away from its manifest meaning. They built their scheme of interpretation on the claim that the Qur'ān contains symbols in the form of words that convey some manifest meanings so that lay Muslims should engage themselves with them. As to the real hidden meanings conveyed by these symbols, this was the exclusive preserve of the "wise men". Thus their cult was built on some notions borrowed from the philosophy of illumination, notions of transmigration and incarnation. It was a mixture of all these notions and some elements borrowed from Judaism, Christianity, some ideas of philosophy and some notions from Zoroastrianism. They believed that Allah incarnated Himself in every Prophet, Imām and in the holy places, and that He was similar to His creation. Further, they believe that in every descendant of 'Alī, Allah is incarnated. These people forced an interpretation upon the Qur'ān to fit the principles constructed by them. They introduced many concocted ways of interpreting the Qur'ān in their own typical way. For example, they interpreted the verse: "and on the Heights there will be men" (7:46) that there is a mountain called *al-A'rāf* which is the center of Gnostic people "who recognize everyone by his marks" (7:46). Similarly, they have explained the verse: "not one of you but will pass over it" (19:71), by saying that "none will reach Allah without crossing over false ideas either during his childhood or after that, then God will save whomsoever He will". The verse of the Qur'ān: "Go, you and your brother to Pharaoh, for he has indeed crossed all bounds" (20:43) to them means: "Pharaohs of one's heart."

Imām Ghazālī took up their refutation in his work titled: *al-Mustaẓhirī*. He says: "if we speak of the esoteric then the esoteric is not subject to any system. Rather it is nothing but subjective thoughts that conflict with each other. This makes it possible to apply the same verse in diverse ways. Those who rely on the esoteric sense could be refuted by a counter meaning and the claim that this was the inner meaning rather than theirs. It is the exoteric manifest meaning which does not admit conflicting views because it is based on the language evolving before the revelation. But in esoteric interpretation no one can establish any argument against the others except if it is supposed by them that any interpretation cannot be received except on the authority of an infallible Imām. And I think this is what these people believe."[1]

This view of Imām Ghazālī is supported by what is found in some of the Ismā'īlis' writings. They say: "shift to an alternative (meaning) is justified when the original is absent. And reflection *(naẓar)* is an alternative to a report. The speech of Allah is the origin. And Allah created man and taught him eloquence. The Imām is the successor of Allah. And in the presence of the successor who explains His speech, there could be no shift to reflection". Ibn al-'Arabī has also exposed in his work *al-'Awāsim* many of their schools' scandalous ideas.[2] This occasion does not permit going into any detail about them. As to a report attributed to Ibn 'Abbās that he said: 'there is a face of the Qur'ān and there is an essence to it',[3] he had himself explained his purport in the following words: 'the appearance of the Qur'ān is its word and the essence is its meaning'.[4] The esoteric *tafsīr* is found in many works including the *Tafsīr* by al-Qāshānī and many of their views are scattered in the treatises of Ikhwān al-Ṣafā (*Rasā'il Ikhwān al-Ṣafā*).

However, it may be borne in mind that what some of the esoteric minded Sufis talk about regarding some verses and assign certain meanings to the words of the Qur'ān over and above their explicit connotations through an interpretation, these meanings are not claimed to be a *tafsīr* of the Qur'ān by these people. What they mean is that,

---

1 Abū Ḥāmid al-Ghazālī, *Faḍā'iḥ al-Bāṭiniyyah*, 'Abd al-Raḥmān Badawī, ed. (Cairo: al-Dār al-Qawmiyyah li al-Ṭibā'at wa al-Nashr, 1383/1964). The complete title of this work is *Faḍā'iḥ al-Bāṭiniyyah wa Faḍā'il al-Mustaẓhiriyyah.* The above mentioned quote from Ibn 'Āshūr however does not occur in the *Faḍā'ih*, rather in al-Ghazālī's *Iḥyā' 'Ulum al-Dīn* (Beirut: Dār al-Ma'rifah, n.d.), 1: 37. (Ed.)

2 Al-Qāḍī Abū Bakr Muḥammad bin 'Abd Allāh bin al-'Arabī, *Kitāb al-'Awāsim min al-Qawāsim*, 1: 43 ff.

3 'Abd al-Raḥmān bin Abī Bakr al-Suyūṭī, *al-Durr al-Manthūr fī al-Tafsīr bi al-Ma'thūr*, 2: 10.

4 Ibid.

that particular verse can be cited to denote the meaning that is being alluded to by the interpreter. It is enough to say in their defense that they have called these interpreted messages as allusions (*ishārāt*) and did not even regard them as meanings. In this way their view becomes different from the position of the *Bāṭiniyyah* referred to above. The true scholars of Islam have taken two positions about them:

i) Imām Ghazālī considers it acceptable. He says in one of the sections of his work *Iḥyā'*: "if you take the statement of the Prophet (peace be upon him): 'the angels do not enter a house where there is a dog or a picture' literally, then this is the exoteric meaning of the statement. The esoteric meaning of this statement will be 'that the heart is a house where angels descend and which is the center of their traces. And the evil habits like anger, low passion, jealousy, hatred and vanity are dogs that bark in the heart. Therefore, angels do not enter a heart filled with these dogs. And the Divine light is not supplied to a heart except through angels. Hence a heart such as this will not receive the supply of light." Thereafter, Imām Ghazālī adds: "I do not mean to say that the word 'house' in this *ḥadīth* means heart and that dog means the evil habit. But I do say that these words of *ḥadīth* should alert us to this aspect of the matter as well."[1] Through this fine distinction, Imām Ghazālī has abandoned the path of *Bāṭiniyyah*. Similar to this is explaining a general verse by some particular aspect of its offshoots. An example of this is found in the section on battles *(al-maghāzī)* in the *Ṣāḥīḥ* of al-Bukhārī. He relates from 'Umar bin 'Aṭā' concerning the verse: "have you not turned your thought to those who exchange the favor of Allah with ingratitude *(kufr)*" (14:28) that these are the people of Quraysh, since Muḥammad (peace be upon him) is indeed a Divine favor.[2] And he added about the end of the same verse

1 Muḥammad bin Muḥammad al-Ghazālī, *Iḥyā' 'Ulūm al-Dīn*, 1: 49.

2 Muḥammad bin Ismā'īl al-Bukhārī, *Ṣaḥīḥ al-Bukhārī*, 675, ḥadīth no. 3977.

(14:28): “they caused their people to descend to the house of perdition” that ‘this was the day of Badr’.[1]

ii) Ibn al-‘Arabī however, in his work *al-‘Awāṣim* thinks that all these allusions and esoteric inferences were baseless. After mentioning the sect of *Bāṭiniyyah* and the treatises of the brethren of *al-Ṣafā’ (Rasā’il Ikhwān al-Ṣafā’)* he said in absolute terms that there could be no inner meaning to the Qur’ān apart from its manifest meaning.[2] So much so that after paying tribute to Imām Ghazālī for his refutation of the *Bāṭiniyyah* and the Philosophers, he added: “Indeed Abū Ḥamid was a full moon that shone in the darkness of nights. He had been a pearl in the jewels of greatness until he entered the realm of *taṣawwuf* and had an excessive engagement with its people. Then he went out of the realm of the reality and deviated in many of his views from the path.”[3]

In my view, these esoteric allusions do not exceed the following three dimensions:

i) the meaning of a verse is comparable to a state corresponding to that meaning. For example, they say concerning the verse: “who could be more wrongful than the one who prevents the mosques of Allāh from remembering His Name in them” (2:114), that there is an allusion in it to the hearts that are places of surrender to Allah, the Almighty. The hearts prostrate before Him by the extinction of egos. Preventing hearts from His remembrance is to block the conferment of spiritual knowledge. The above verse also says afterwards “… and struggled for their destruction”. This alludes to “contaminating the hearts by prejudices and stray passions.”

---

1 Ibid.

2 Al-Qāḍī Abū Bakr Muḥammad bin ‘Abd Allāh bin al-‘Arabī, *Kitāb al-‘Awāsim min al-Qawāsim*, 1: 121 ff.

3 Ibid., 1: 85.

The situation mentioned in the verse is comparable to one who does not purify his soul by knowledge and thus prevents his heart from attaining qualities of perfection that come with that knowledge. Referring to this verse in that state of spiritual emptiness is like using a proverbial phrase. Similar is their view about the esoteric meaning of the tradition: “angels do not enter a house in which there is a dog”, as mentioned before with reference to Imām al-Ghazālī.

ii) a sort of optimistic inference from a word or phrase that draws attention of the listener to something that is occupying his mind. For example, someone who said that in the verse: “who is there who could intercede ...” (2:255), the word: *man dha’lladhī* draws attention to the soul to become among those intercessors who are in the proximity of Allah. This is an instance of attention being drawn to a thought occupying the listener’s mind.

iii) lessons and messages drawn by those men whose minds are alive and who are ever prepared to benefit from everything, take heed and derive wisdom from wherever it is found. One could well imagine the state of heart and soul experienced when those who, when they recite the Qur’ān, deliberate over it, and heed to its lessons, hear the verse: “But Pharaoh disobeyed the messenger, so we seized him with a heavy punishment” (73:16), they infer from it the message that a heart which does not follow the Prophet who is a carrier of higher knowledge is doomed to disaster. An anecdote will further explain this aspect: “someone passed by a man who was saying to somebody: ‘this wood (tree) is fruitless. It is only fit for fire: He started crying and said: ‘then a fruitless heart is also fit for nothing except fire’.”

Therefore, attributing an allusion to the text of the Qur’ān is only figurative because it indicates a mental preparedness and reflective response of some people who are in either of the three states mentioned above. Since the verses of the Qur'ān enlighten their reflection and incite a receptiveness to take lesson, they attribute this allusion to the verse. This allusion is by no means considered a semantic connotation of the word integral to the word and its auxiliaries as we have clarified before. And whatever allusion exceeds the limits of the abovementioned three states then gradually enters the sphere of *bāṭiniyyah* until it assumes their typical doctrinal scope. We have already explained the frontiers and fault lines dividing the two approaches. Whenever you traverse the intersection between the two approaches, you should ascertain its underlying idea and you have the touchstone whereby you can avoid entering the wrong field.

However, the allusion we are talking about does not include implied connotation (*dalālat al-Ishārah*), substance of the address (*faḥwa al-khiṭāb*), the inclusiveness (*istighrāq*), of the definite article, or implication by association (*dalālat al-taḍammun*) or corollary *(iltizām)* that the scholars have deduced from the Qur'ān in order to develop arguments for validating injunctions. An example of this deduction is to argue for the validity of agency *(wakāla)* from the verse: "now send one of you with this money of yours" (18:19), or the permissibility of guarantees from the words of the Qur'ān: "and I will be bound by it" (12:72) or the validity of analogy from the verse: "… that you might judge between people by that which Allah has shown you" (4:105). Nor does allusion include metaphorical meanings of verses like: "O mountains! Echo back the praise of Allah with him!" (34:10) and: "He said to it and to the earth: Come together willingly or unwillingly. They said we do come in willing obedience" (41:11). Nor does it include forms of the text in which a condition takes the place of speech like in the verse: "There is not a thing but celebrates His praise and yet you understand not how they celebrate His glory" (17:44). All the above examples represent replacing the usage with a linguistic construction. The consensus of the Arabs over these constructions is well established. Therefore, these are recognized as extended semantic significations.

Al-Zamakhsharī says in *al-Kashshāf*: "there are so many verses revealed in respect of non-believers, but there is great deal of matter in them for reflection by the believers and for taking lessons from their contexts."[1] What he meant was that these verses relate to the non-believers according to their direct signification but also touch upon the condition of believers by way of indirect allusion.

I deem it my religious duty to warn the Muslims against something that they regard as ordinary but which is a serious matter in the sight of Allah. This duty impels me to caution them against explaining or interpreting the Book without relying on the celebrated *mufassirīn*. They should not even attempt to say anything by way of interpretation or explanation from any source unless the author of that source is fully competent and qualified on the basis of his expertise in those sciences that we have enumerated in the second part of this introduction.

Many people have been going off the mark in explaining the verses of the Qur'ān. Therefore, it is the obligation of every intelligent man to appreciate the worth and value of this formidable field of study. He should abide by its framework of principles and should refer everything to the authoritative sources in this field. This is necessary to keep distinction between the genuine and the fake so that one does not grope in utter darkness. The silence of scholars over these omissions increases indulgence by people in these blunders, and they lose sight of their destination; it is the duty of scholars to show the way and rectify the mistakes.

---

1 Maḥmūd bin 'Umar al-Zamakhsharī, *al-Kashshāf*, 4: 379.

CHAPTER FOUR

WHAT OUGHT TO BE THE AIM OF THE *MUFASSIR*?

After talking about the sources of *tafsīr*, validity of *tafsīr* without transmitted reports, cautioning against the so-called esoteric *tafsīr* and its distinction from allusions, the readers should expect some elaboration of the aims of a *mufassir* in his *tafsīr*. We shall be talking about the objectives for the statement of which the Qur'ān has been revealed. This will put in relief the purpose which the scholars of *tafsīr* have sought to achieve through their works in different ways. This will enable you to assess the degree of success achieved by a *mufassir* in attaining these objectives. Then we will be talking about the instances of deviation from these objectives and adherence to them in the works of *tafsīr*. At the end of this section, we will highlight the deductions by the scholars from the Qur'ān to enrich numerous sciences.

The Qur'ān has been sent down by Allah Almighty for improving and reforming the affairs of the entire humanity as a mercy unto them and to convey to them their *raison d'etre*. God Almighty says: "and we have sent down the Book to you explaining all things, a guide, a mercy, and glad tidings to Muslims" (16:89). Therefore, the highest objective of the Qur'ān was to reform the individual, collective and cultural conditions of human life. Reform of the individual rests on taming the self and purifying it. The crux of this matter is the reform of basic beliefs. Because these are the sources of upright thinking and moral rectitude. Thereafter comes the reform of purely personal and intimate aspects of life. The latter depends on the outer forms of worship such as the prayers and the inner dimensions of it like adorning oneself with the renunciation of jealousy, hatred and vanity. As to the collective reform, it is first attained by individuals' reform since the individuals are the constituents of the society. No collectivity could improve without reforming its individual parts. And there is something more that is needed. This is to regulate the dealings of people with each other in a way that protects them against courting lower passions and succumbing to baser instincts. The latter is called the science of transactions. Some philosophers have named it civic management or social organization. As to the socio-cultural reform, it is wider than the former since it protects the order in the Islamic world and regulates the mutual dealings of various groups and territories in such a manner that protects the interests of all. It also upholds the general Islamic weal and protects the collective purpose of cohesion when some minor interest shows resistance. This is called the science of culture and society.

The purpose of Allah in revealing His Book is to explain the modes of behavior that lead to the protection of the objectives of religion. He has incorporated this message in the text of the Qur'ān whereby He addressed us in clear, emphatic terms. He has also prescribed for us the acquisition of knowledge and awareness of this message as part of our religious duty. Says He: "here is a Book which we have sent down unto you, full of blessings that they may meditate on its verses and that men of understanding may receive admonition" (38:29). Whether we say that it is possible to attain all the knowledge of Allah's purpose revealed in His Book, as contented by our scholars as well as by al-Mashā'ikhī and al-Sakkākī, from amongst the *Mu'tazilah*, or take the view of the rest of the *Mu'tazilah* that it was not possible to encompass all the knowledge of Allah's purpose[1] – though this is a fruitless controversy – the main intention on our part remains unchanged. That is to attain this knowledge within the limits of the practical possibility – not the logical possibility. Therefore, there is no bar to recognizing the obligation to exhaust our search for the Divine purpose to the utmost of our ability

1 Muḥammad bin 'Abd Allāh al-Zarkashī, *al-Burhān fī 'Ulūm al-Qur'ān*, Muḥammad Abū al-Faḍl Ibrāhīm, ed., 2nd ed. (Beirut: Dār al-Ma'rifah li al-Ṭibā'ah wa al-Nashr, n.d.), 2: 99-100.

and capacity for this knowledge – even though a complete knowledge might be difficult to attain.

Allah Almighty has chosen to clothe His Revelation in the dress of Arabic language. This language is the vehicle of His message. He has also willed that the Arab people should be the first recipients of His law and His message in His Infinite Wisdom known to Himself. Among the reasons for this choice is that the Arabic language is the most eloquent medium and easiest of dissemination. It has the highest capacity to carry and convey the meaning with brevity and precision. Another reason is that the community which is chosen as the recipient should be one that remained immune from hairsplittings in disputes and dialectics. Nor should this community be such as has been exhausted by an obsessive pursuit of material prosperity and thus held back from the attainment of real greatness and nobility since the former pursuit often weakens this urge.

However, it is essential to know in absolute terms that the meaning of addressing the Arabs with the Qur'ān is not that the prescriptions of the Qur'ān are confined to them or take into account only their particular circumstances. Because the universality of the *sharī'ah* and its permanent character and the abiding miracle of the Qur'ān down the stream of time controverts that supposition. The objectives of the Qur'ān undoubtedly include cleaning of their souls because they were chosen by God to receive His message and disseminate it. They were the primary addressees before the rest of the community was called upon to join the mission. Therefore, consideration was definitely given to their conditions. A great deal of the Qur'ān was, therefore, intentionally addressed to them and to the reform of their conditions. The Qur'ān says:

"lest you should say: the Book was sent down to two peoples before us and We remained unacquainted with all that they learned by assiduous study or lest you should say: if the Book had only been sent down to us We should have followed its guidance better than they" (6:156-7).

However, this was by no means meant to confine the address to them, as we will explain later.

It is, therefore, necessary to know the original objectives for the elaboration of which the Qur'ān came. These objectives, in our view, consist of the following eight points.

(i) Reform of belief and teaching the right belief. This is the highest means of reforming mankind. Because it removes from the mind the tendency to surrender to anything without an established reason. It cleanses the heart from the superstitions of polytheism and atheism and what comes between the two. The Qur'ān refers to this fact when it says: "The deities, other than God, whom they invoked, profited them no whit when there issued the decree of your Lord nor did they add aught to their lot but perdition" (11:101). To their false deities was attributed their added perdition, though this was not the act of the deities but a result of their believing in them.

(ii) Reform of morals. God Almighty says: "And thou (standest) on an exalted standard of character" (68:04). 'Ā'ishah, while explaining this verse, said, when she was asked about the morals of the Prophet (peace be upon him): "his morals were the Qur'ān."[1] In a tradition related by Imām Mālik in *al-Muwaṭṭa'*, one finds the following message: "I have been sent to perfect moral qualities."[2] This objective of the Qur'ān was clearly understood by the Arabs, especially the Prophet's companions.

(iii) Prescribing injunctions, both general and particular. The Qur'ān says: "We have sent down to thee the Book in truth,

1 Aḥmad bin Muḥammad bin Ḥanbal, *al-Musnad*, Ḥamzah Aḥmad al-Zayn, ed., 17:379, ḥadīth no. 24482. The editor says about this ḥadīth, "Its *isnād* (chain) is authentic." See, ibid., footnote no. 24482.

2 Mālik bin Anas, *al-Muwaṭṭa'*, 2: 904.

that thou mightest judge between men, as guided by Allah: so be not (used) as an advocate by those who betray their trust" (4:105), and it says: "To thee We sent the Scripture in truth, confirming the scripture that came before it, and guarding it in safety: so judge between them by what Allah hath revealed" (5:48). The Qur'ān has set forth most of the injunctions in general terms. It has also provided particular details in important matters. When it says: "*explaining all things*" (16:89) and "this day I have perfected your Religion" (5:3), it means perfecting the general principles.

(iv) Socio-political order of the community. This is a great theme of the Qur'ān that aims at the reform and rectitude of the community and preservation of its order. For example, it provides guidance to form unity in the ranks. It says: "And hold fast, all together, by the rope which Allah (stretches out for you), and be not divided among yourselves; and remember with gratitude Allah's favor on you; for ye were enemies and He joined your hearts in love, so that by His Grace, ye became brethren; and ye were on the brink of the pit of Fire, and He saved you from it" (3:103) and "As for those who divide their religion and break up into sects, thou hast no part in them in the least" (6:159) and "and fall into no disputes, lest ye lose heart and your power depart" (8:46) and "who (conduct) their affairs by mutual consultation" (42:38).

(v) Stories and annals of the past peoples of history to emulate their good examples of conduct. The Qur'ān says: "We do relate unto thee the most beautiful of stories, in that We reveal to thee this (portion of the) Qur'ān: before this, thou too were among those who knew it not" (12:3) and "Those were the (prophets) who received Allah's guidance: Follow the guidance they received"(6:90) and to warn against their evil deeds, it says: "ye were clearly shown how We dealt with them; and We put forth (many) parables in your behoof!" (14:45).

All these stories contain teachings as we have mentioned in the second part of this introduction.

(vi) Teaching, according to the condition of the addressees' age, whatever enables them to receive the *sharī'ah* and disseminate it. This teaching should consist of the science of Divine laws and the knowledge of transmitted traditions. This had been the level of knowledge of those Arabs who had occasion to mix with Arab Christians. The Qur'ān added to this content the teaching of the wisdom of the standards of reasoning and sound argument. This was done in the context of its dialectics with the straying people and was reiterated by the stress of the Qur'ān on reflective thinking. It said: "He granteth wisdom to whom He pleaseth; and he to whom wisdom is granted receiveth indeed a benefit overflowing" (2:269).

Indeed this was the vast source from which sprang fountains of profound knowledge that opened the sights of the unlettered people to knowledge. This was reinforced by frequent emphasis on the benefits of knowledge. This was the kind of knowledge the Arabs were not familiar with. Their utmost knowledge consisted of experience. Their wise men were men whose exceptional intelligence was augmented by practical experience. These were the ones known as men of knowledge among the Arabs people. They have been referred to in the verses of the Qur'ān as "men of knowledge". The Qur'ān says, for example: "but only those understand them who have knowledge" (29:43) and "Say: Are those equal, those who know and those who do not know?" (39:9). And it says: "*Nun*. By the Pen and the (Record) which (men) write" (68:1). In the latter verse, the Qur'ān emphasized the value of the skill of writing.

(vii) Preaching and warning, cautioning and giving glad tidings. This element is contained in all those verses that deal with promises and warnings *(wa'd* and *wa'īd)*. Also the verses that contain dialectics and argumentation with the opponents deal with this theme. All these themes together constitute the subject matter of encouragement and dissuasion.

(viii) Revealing the miraculous character of the Qur'ān to provide a sign showing the truthfulness of the Prophet (peace be upon him). This is because declaring his truthfulness depends upon the testimony of the miracle following the open challenge of the Qur'ān in this regard. The Qur'ān combines in itself dual qualities of miraculousness. It is both a miracle of words and meanings and it contains a challenge to that effect. It says: "Say: 'Bring then a Sūra like unto it'" (10:38). The knowledge about the occasions of revelation (*asbāb al-nuzūl*) also provides help in showing the requirement of the context in which a certain verse or verses have been revealed. The latter in turn helps us in appreciating the stylistic miracle of the Book since its style is in conformity with the requirements of the context.

This, in a nutshell, is what I have understood to be the objectives of the Revelation. Imām Ghazālī in his *Iḥyā' 'Ulūm al-Dīn* also has something to say on this subject.[1]

Therefore, the primary aim of a *mufassir* is to explain what he understands to be the purport of God Almighty in His Book. He should adequately explain whatever its meaning contains. This meaning should be permitted by the semantics of the words employed in the Book. At the same time, this explanation should bring out the sense of the words in terms of the objectives of the Qur'ān. It should also embrace those ideas that enable one to fully grasp the meaning and message of the Book. Or the *mufassir* should highlight the objectives of the Qur'ān in a detailed and applied manner with reference to the meaning supplied by its verses, as we explained in the first section of this Introduction. Where he finds some vagueness, he should clearly establish its meaning

1 See, Muḥammad bin Muḥammad al-Ghazālī, *Iḥyā' 'Ulūm al-Dīn*, 1: 281-95.

based on valid argument. He should also clarify the correct meaning wherever he apprehends an erroneous claim by any prejudiced or ignorant person and this clarification should also be supported by valid argument.

An overall understanding of the objectives for which the Qur'ān has been sent down should, therefore, be the main guide of a *mufassir* in his endeavors. He should also be conversant with the Qur'ānic terms of reference in the use of words and expressions because Revelation follows its own terms and conventions. The author of *al-Kashshāf* has dealt with the manners of these conventions of the Qur'ān and his discussion in this regard is scattered throughout this work.

The modes of the scholars of the Qur'ān are, in the main, three:

(i) They confine themselves to the manifest meaning that is originally attached to the construction of words and then they elaborate and explain it further. This was originally the task taken up by the *mufassirūn*.

(ii) They derive meanings beyond the manifest as implied by the semantics of the words or indicated by the context. However, these extended meanings are neither against Arabic usage nor do they run contrary to the objectives of the Qur'ān. But these are consequential nuances of constructions that are the traits of Arabic language. The science of Rhetoric and Stylistics has explained these traits. For example, they say that an accentuated stress is indicative of a denial or reluctance on the part of the listener. Hence the stress. Other examples include the "core and substance of the address" (*faḥwa al-Khiṭāb*), an implied connotation and the possibility of metaphor along with the literal sense. Or else he may bring such other issues into his elaborate discussion as they have a nexus with the meanings of the verses, or because a clear understanding of the meaning of the Qur'ān depends on a clear understanding of those issues. He may also do so to show the concord between the meaning of the Qur'ānic text and the sciences dealing with these issues and to highlight their overall link with the objectives of prescribing the injunctions. This is done for the sake of added emphasis on these injunctions. The scholars of the Qur'ān also introduce these extended discussions in their works in order to refute the contention of those who think that these conclusions are in conflict with the Qur'ān. However, the scholars do not discuss these issues on the claim that these matters were directly the purport of the verses of the Qur'ān, but they do this for the sake of an exhaustive discussion of all the relevant issues. We have already alluded to this fact in the second section of this Introduction.

(iii) In the second mode of *tafsīr* adopted by the scholars, they show detailed application of the Qur'ān in terms of the injunctions derived from it. They have focused on these injunctions in their extensive works of *tafsīr*. They also go into a detailed discussion of moral and ethical principles and their applications in life. For example, Imām Ghazālī has discussed these things a great deal.[1] Therefore, a *mufassir* cannot be blamed for bringing in a detailed application of Qur'ānic injunctions as reflected in various Islamic sciences because these serve the supreme objectives of the Qur'ān, and because these have a nexus with matters Islamic. For example, suppose a *mufassir* might explain the words of the Qur'ān "and to Moses Allah spoke directly" (4:164) in the light of the theologians' discussions about establishing the "inner speech" (*al-kalām al-nafsī*) and might produce arguments in support of this doctrine. Similarly, he could talk about the words of the Qur'ān and their status in light of the views of various theological schools. In the same way, a scholar may bring the

---

1 See, Muḥammad bin Muḥammad al-Ghazālī, *Iḥyā' 'Ulūm al-Dīn*.

etiquettes of the teacher and the learner while explaining the story of Prophet Mūsā (peace be upon him) with al-Khiḍr related in the Qur'ān, as was done by Imām Ghazālī.[1] Similarly, we find Ibn al-'Arabī saying that he had dictated eight hundred issues derived from this story of the Qur'ān. Also may be included in such extended discussion legal issues emanating from the words of the Qur'ān: "... then from a sperm-drop, then from a leech-like clot" (40:67). Because such a discussion would be related to the objectives of the Qur'ān and it will further affirm the grandness of Divine creative power.

(iv) In the third mode of *tafsīr*, such academic issues are drawn into discussions that have a link with the purpose of a verse. This is done either because some of these issues have been alluded to by the meaning of that verse even if it is an implicit allusion. For example, someone might explain the verse "and he to whom wisdom is granted receiveth indeed a benefit overflowing" (2:269), and bring up the subject of the classification of *ḥikmah* and its benefits admitting it under the words: *"khayran kathīra"*. While *ḥikmah* is a formal category of knowledge and is not included in the fullness of the meaning of this verse, detailing the categories of *ḥikmah* does help in appreciating the message of the verse without compromising the original meaning. Likewise, we could talk about details of political economy and distribution of wealth under the rubric of the verse: "in order that it may not (merely) make a circuit between the wealthy among you" (59:7), and explain it in terms of the prescribed institutions of *zakāt*, inheritance and the transactions consisting of capital and labor since this verse does make slight allusion to all this.

There are indeed certain academic issues that have a close link with the explanation of verses of the Qur'ān. For example, some scholars

---

1 Muḥammad bin Muḥammad al-Ghazālī, *Iḥyā' 'Ulūm al-Dīn*, 1: 51.

might bring up the theological issue of establishing the argument of 'mutual exclusiveness' (*tamānu'*) in his elaboration of the verse: "If there were, in the heavens and the earth, other gods besides Allah, there would have been confusion in both" (21:22). Another one could explain the verse: "With power and skill did We construct the Firmament" (51:47) and discuss the issue of *mutashābih* (figurative statement of transcendental realities). Obviously, these issues do have a relation with the aims of *tafsīr*.

Likewise, the purpose of the following verse of the Qur'ān: "Do they not look at the sky above them? How We have made it and adorned it, and there are no flaws in it?" (50:6) is, no doubt, taking lessons from observing this phenomenon. But if a *mufassir* adds details of this phenomenon and elaborates its deeper meanings and the cause and effect system going through this phenomenon, – facts explained in the science of Astronomy – such a scholar does indeed advance the cause of *tafsīr* further.

At times, a scholar of *tafsīr* discusses certain issues in order to show a concordance and conformity between the meaning of the Qur'ān and the established facts of empirical science. On some occasions, a scholar tries to derive certain things about the end of the world from the Qur'ān. For example, deriving the idea that the end of this world will be through earthquakes from the verse: "One Day We shall remove the mountains" (18:47) and to discover the notion that at the end of the world, the system of earth's gravity will be disturbed from the verse: "When the sun (with its spacious light) is folded up" (81:1). The condition for all the above discussions to be acceptable in *tafsīr* is that these should be concise. Only the jist of the findings of the relevant science should be produced casually and this sort of discussion should never be attempted *per se*, nor should these be presented as something integral to the purpose of the Revelation.

In respect of adopting this third mode, the scholars generally maintain the following views.

There is a group of scholars who consider it worthy to show a conformity between the non-religious sciences and their tools and the meanings of the Qur'ān. They find the Qur'ān pointing to many aspects of such conformity. Ibn Rushd, the grandson, says in his work: *Faṣl al-Maqāl*: "Muslims are agreed that it is not necessary to assign an explicit meaning to the texts of the *sharī'ah*, nor is it necessary that all words must leave their direct explicit meaning by way of interpretation. The reason for the *sharī'ah* having an exoteric aspect as well as an esoteric dimension is the variety of thinking among people, and the diverse tendencies among them in the matter of accepting and confirming religious tenets."[1] Ibn Rushd reaches the conclusion that there was a link between the sciences of the *sharī'ah* and the sciences of philosophy. In his work *Sharḥ Ḥikmat al-Ishrāq*, Quṭb al-Dīn Shīrāzī has expressed a similar view. Also we find that men like Imām Ghazālī, Imām Rāzī and Abū Bakr bin al-'Arabī have treated this subject extensively. They have accumulated a lot of evidence drawn from rational sciences in favor of the contentions of the Qur'ān. The jurists of Islam have done the same in their works on the legal injunctions of the Qur'ān.

Similarly, Ibn Jinnī, al-Zujāj and Abū Ḥayyān have filled their works of *tafsīr* with abundant argument for the rules of Arabic grammar.[2] There is, however, little doubt that the speech emanating from The All-Knowing Almighty who transcends all imperfections cannot be constructed on the semantics of a particular group. However,

---

1 Abū al-Walīd bin Rushd, *Faṣl al-Maqāl fīmā bayn al-Ḥikmah wa al-Sharī'at min al-Ittiṣāl*, Muḥammad 'Amārah, ed. (Cairo: Dār al-Ma'ārif, n.d.), 33-34.

2 See, Abū al-Fatḥ 'Uthmān bin Jinnī, *al-Khaṣā'iṣ*, Muḥammad 'Alī al-Najjār, ed. (Cairo: Maṭba'ah Dār al-Kutub al-Miṣriyyah, 1371/1952), 2 vols.; Idem., *Sirr Ṣanā'at al-I'rāb*, Ḥasan Handāwī, ed. (Damascus: Dār al-Qalam, 1405/1985), 2 vols.; al-Zujāj, *I'rāb al-Qur'ān*, Ibrāhīm al-Abyārī, ed. (Cairo: al-Hay'at al-'Āmmah li Shu'ūn al-Maṭābi' al-Amīriyyah, 1963 AD), 3 vols. It is to be noted, however, that the modern editor of this book has cast serious doubts on the authenticity of the attribution of its authorship to al-Zujāj.; Abū Ḥayyān Muḥammad bin Yūsuf, *Tafsīr al-Baḥr al-Muḥīṭ* (Beirut: Dār al-Fikr li al-Ṭibā'ah wa al-Nashr wa al-Tawzī', 1403/1983), 8 vols.

the meanings of His speech do conform to the reality. And therefore, if a facet of reality is found in any science and a verse has a link with that, then this reality is indeed intended in the meaning of that verse to the extent of human capacity to attain its knowledge at present or in future. But this matter differs according to the difference in the level of understanding of each individual. The condition for the validity of such a discussion is that these interpretive meanings should not go outside the scope of Arabic usage. Nor should it depart from the explicit meaning of the Qur'ānic words except on the basis of some evidence or argument. Nor should any meaning that is remote or alien to the original meaning of the word be artificially imposed upon the Qur'ān. Because this will land the *mufassir* in the sphere of the *Bāṭiniyyah*. Abū Isḥāq al-Shāṭibī has something different to say on this issue. He says: "in the matter of comprehending and explaining the Qur'ān, nothing is correct unless it is prevalent among all the Arabs. Whatever thing is beyond their comprehension should not be pressed into the text of the Qur'ān."[1] He further says: "whatever is decided in respect of the *ummī* origin of the *sharī'ah* and that it has proceeded on their pattern i.e. the Arabs, certain principles are based on this premise: Many people have crossed the limits in ascribing ideas to the Qur'ān. They have attributed to it all sorts of past and present science such as physics, logic, science of letters and such other things. However all this does not conform to what we have explained above. Because the pious elders were more informed about the Qur'ān and their sciences and we have no report that any of them ever spoke of any such thing save what is evidently included in its content namely, the injunctions concerning (human) obligations and the matters of the hereafter. Yes, it did contain knowledge that was commensurate with the familiar heritage of the Arabs. This knowledge had bewildered their men of wisdom whose exceptional minds could not attain them".[2]

---

1 Ibrāhīm bin Mūsā al-Shāṭibī, *al-Mawāfaqāt fī Uṣūl al-Sharī'ah*, 'Abd Allāh Darāz, ed., 2nd ed. (Beirut: Dār al-Ma'rifah li al-Ṭibā'ah wa al-Nashr, 1395/1975), 2: 85.

2 Ibid., 2: 79-80.

Al-Shāṭibī has established the above principle on the presumption that since the Qur'ān was an address to the 'unlettered ones' and they were the Arabs, therefore, the mode of comprehending and explaining the Qur'ān should rely on their ability and capacity. He has also presumed the *ummī* origin of the *sharī'ah*.

However, all these premises are quite baseless for the following six reasons.

i. His premise presupposes that the Qur'ān did not take into account any change in the condition of the Arabs and this is a wrong premise, as we have explained above.

ii. The objectives of the Qur'ān aim at the universality of its message. It is an abiding miracle. Therefore, it must contain things that could be understood by those people who will be living in the age of proliferation of science.

iii. The early elders (*salaf*) have asserted that the wonders of the Qur'ān shall appear endlessly. By this they meant its meanings. If things were as opined by al-Shāṭibī, its wonders would have come to an end with the exhaustion of its shades of meanings.

iv. The miraculous quality of the Qur'ān includes the fact that it should contain, despite the conciseness of its words, things that could not be covered by numerous books.

v. the initial capacity of its addressees for comprehending it only requires that the basic meaning should be understood by them. But whatever extends beyond the basic meaning could still be grasped by other peoples while some people might remain oblivious to it as the Prophet (peace be upon him) said: "there may be a carrier of religious knowledge conveying it to those who understand it better than him."[1]

---

1 Abū Ja'far al-Ṭaḥāwī, *Sharḥ Mushkil al-Āthār*, Shu'ayb al-Arna'ūt (ed.) (Beirut: Mu'assasat al-Risālah, 1415 AH), 4/392.

vi. if lack of notice by the early elders (*salaf*) concerns matters that do not relate to the objectives of the Qur'ān, then we support this stand. But if it concerns things that are relevant to its objectives, then we do not accept that they were confined to the apparent meanings of the verses. On the contrary, they did explain and expand the meanings and implications of verses showing their applications in the sciences with which they had been concerned. And this should not deter us from following their footsteps in other sciences that are related to the objectives of the Qur'ān and serve them and show the vast expanses of the Islamic sciences. Whatever is beyond that scope, if it is intended to elaborate the meaning then this is related with *tafsīr* as well. Because the rational sciences actually discuss the conditions of things as they exist. If a discussion exceeds that purview, then this is not part of *tafsīr* but only a kind of supplement to complete the relevant academic discussion, or it is a reference to something that has a nexus with the *tafsīr*. This is done to expand the academic range of the students of *tafsīr*.

To sum up the discussion, I would say that the relation of various sciences with the Qur'ān is at four levels:

(i) sciences contained in the Qur'ān such as the annals of the prophets and past communities, reform of morals, laws and legislation, beliefs, principles of the *sharī'ah*, Arabic language and Rhetoric;

(ii) sciences that add to the knowledge of the *mufassir* like philosophy, astronomy and the knowledge about the characteristics of creatures;

(iii) sciences to which there is some allusion in the Qur'ān or which have provided some support to its contentions like geology, medicine and logic;

(v) sciences that have no relation to the Qur'ān, either because they are false like mythology and things related to it, or because they provide no help to serve the purpose of the Qur'ān like prosody and rhymes.

CHAPTER FIVE

ON THE OCCASIONS OF REVELATION

Many scholars of *tafsīr* have gone to great lengths to find out the occasions of the revelation of the Qur'ānic verses. These occasions are those events about which it is reported that certain verses of the Qur'ān have been revealed in connection with them to lay down an injunction for them, to narrate them or to express disapprobation for them. They have cited these reports so excessively that it has made people think that every verse has been revealed in connection with an occasion. They have gone to the extent of undermining trust in their reporting of these events. No doubt, however, that there are found in some verses a reference to the occasion that has invited their revelation. And we do find for some verses occasions that have been established by reports free from the possibility that these were the opinions of their reporters. We, therefore, feel that the matter of citing these reports should stand between the two extremes. Hence there is a great detriment to the understanding of the Qur'ān in both ignoring these reports altogether and admitting them in their entirety.

It was thus necessary to delve into this issue because it requires careful investigation during the process of interpretation. And I will try to state a view about it that will cover all its dimensions. We should here give an allowance to the early scholars who have written a great deal on the occasions of the Revelation because every writer feels an urge to expand the range of his subject so as to cover all the available material. However, I find no excuse for the great authorities on *tafsīr* who have uncritically accumulated a lot of weak reports in their works without clarifying their authenticity or otherwise. They have thereby given an impression that the verses of the Qur'ān were revealed only due to certain events inviting their revelation. And this is a wrong supposition because the Qur'ān has come as a guide for the Ummah in different fields. Therefore, its revelation did not have to depend on events inviting prescription of injunctions. No doubt, the scholars have been making it clear that an occasion of revelation does not qualify or limit the importance of a verse to that occasion.[1] Though there has been a minority view that the occasions do qualify and limit.[2] Even if there were occasions of revelation related to all the general verses, this would have application because the scholars of jurisprudence have already solved this problem to our relief by laying down the maxim: "it is the generality of the text which matters and not the particularity of the occasion."[3] Still there are many occasions the reporters of which have intended thereby to determine the purport by qualifying a general statement or making an unconditional statement contingent upon a condition or assigning a certain meaning to the text in any other way. It is these kinds of occasions that stand in need of evaluation before any attempt to determine the meaning of the Qur'ān.

In the beginning of his work on the occasions of the Revelation, al-Wāḥīdī says: "and today everyone is fabricating an occasion for the verse inventing all sorts of lies and false attributions lending himself to ignorance without being mindful of the warning in this regard."[4] He adds: "it is wrong to speak of the occasions of Revelation without proper transmission and hearing from those who witnessed the Revelation."[5]

There are certain occasions the knowledge of which is indispensable for the scholar of the Qur'ān. Because these elaborate the brief statements and explain the hidden meanings. There are even some occasions that in themselves provide the relevant *tafsīr*. There are others that guide the scholars of *tafsīr* to search for those arguments

1 Jalāl al-Dīn 'Abd al-Raḥmān al-Suyūṭī, *al-Itqān*, 1: 95-96.

2 Ibid.

3 Ibid.

4 'Alī bin Aḥmad al-Wāḥidī, *Asbāb Nuzūl al-Qur'ān*, al-Sayyid Aḥmad Ṣaqar, ed. (n.p.: Dār al-Kitāb al-Jadīd, 1389/1969), 5-6.

5 Ibid., 5.

that provide the relevant explanation or interpretation. It has been reported by al-Bukhārī in his *Ṣaḥīḥ* that Marwān bin al-Ḥakam (the first Umayyad Caliph) sent for 'Abd Allāh bin 'Abbās to enquire about the verse: "Think not that those who exult in what they have brought about, and love to be praised for what they have not done, shall escape the penalty. For them is a penalty grievous indeed" (3:188), asking him the following question: "if everyone who is proud of his doings and desirous of praise for doing nothing is going to be punished, then are not all of us going to be punished? Ibn 'Abbās replied: "in fact the Prophet (peace be upon him) had once called the Jews to ask them a question to which they replied wrongly concealing the truth of the matter. Thereupon, this verse was revealed condemning them for concealing the truth and yet being proud of this act and further desiring praise even on this wrong-doing of theirs." Thereafter, Ibn 'Abbās recited the verse before it to clarify the meaning and the context. This verse is as follows: "And remember Allah took a covenant from the People of the Book, to make it known and clear to mankind, and not to hide it; but they threw it away behind their backs, and purchased with it some miserable gain! And vile was the bargain they made! Think not that those who exult in what they have brought about, and love to be praised for what they have not done, shall escape the penalty. For them is a penalty grievous indeed" (3:187, 188).[1]

Similarly, as partly referred to above, *al-Muwaṭṭa'* relates the report of 'Urwah bin Zubayr who had asked 'Ā'ishah (may God be pleased with her) about the verse: "Behold! Safa and Marwa are among the Symbols of Allah. So if those who visit the House in the Season or at other times, should compass them round, it is no sin in them" (2:158). Asked whether it suggested that someone could leave this 'running' between Ṣafā and Marwah, 'Ā'ishah (may God be pleased with her) replied that if this were so, it should have been said: ".... there is no blame if he does not run."[2] "In fact," 'Ā'ishah (may God be pleased

1 Muḥammad bin Ismā'īl al-Bukhārī, *Ṣaḥīḥ al-Bukhārī*, 779, ḥadīth no. 4568.

2 Mālik bin Anas, *al-Muwaṭṭa'*, 1: 273.

with her) added, "this verse was revealed with reference to those of *Anṣār* who used to extol *Manāt* and to refrain from running between *Ṣafā* and *Marwah*. When Islam came, they asked the Prophet (peace be upon him) about it, whereupon this verse was revealed."[1]

Among the occasions of the revelation that help explain the meaning of the Qur'ān are those that draw the attention of the scholars of *tafsīr* to certain rhetorical features in the light of the requirement of the context. There are so many occasions that portray the situation, which, in turn, helps us appreciate rhetorical qualities of the relevant verses.

I have surveyed the occasions of revelation the reports of which are authentic. I found them made up of five categories.

(i) That which is the purpose of a verse, the meaning of which could only be understood with its knowledge. It is, therefore, necessary for the scholar to look for it. This category includes the vague statements of the Qur'ān, like the verse: "Allah has indeed heard (and accepted) the statement of the woman who pleads with thee concerning her husband" (58:1), the verse: "O ye of Faith! Say not (to the Messenger) words of ambiguous import, but words of respect" (2:104) and like some verses that start with the words "there are some people who ..."

(ii) That in which an event has given rise to the prescription of some injunctions. The forms of these events do not explain any brief statement, nor do they go against the import of the verse by way of qualification, generalization or limitation. However, if similar events are mentioned, they appear commensurate with the import of the verses. An example of this is the report of 'Uwaymir al-'Ajlānī concerning whom the verse of *li'ān* (swearing between spouses on alleged adultery) was revealed[2] or the report of Ka'b bin 'Ujrah, in

1 Ibid.

2 Muḥammad bin Ismā'īl al-Bukhārī, *Ṣaḥīḥ al-Bukhārī*, 939, ḥadīth no. 5259.

whose case the verse "and if any of you is ill, or has an ailment in his scalp (necessitating shaving), (he should) in compensation either fast, or feed the poor, or offer sacrifice" (2:196) was revealed. Ka'b bin 'Ujrah used to say afterwards: "this verse was for me particularly and for you generally."[1] Another example of this is the remark of Umm Salamah (may God be pleased with her) to the Prophet (peace be upon him): "the men fight but we do not" whereupon the following verse was revealed: "Do not covet that whereby God in bounty has preferred one of you above another" (4:32).[2] In this category, a notice of the occasion helps only in a better comprehension of the meaning of the verse and in finding an illustration for the injunction contained in the verse. There is no risk involved that the occasion might restrict the injunction to that event. Because the scholars have almost agreed that in such cases, the occasion does not serve as a qualifier. There is a consensus among the scholars that the essence of a legislative injunction is that it is not specific in its application.

(iii) Events relating to individuals that are numerous. The verse is revealed in this category to announce something, lay down injunctions concerning the event or rebuke someone on account of committing something related to that event. Often we find the scholars of *tafsīr* saying: 'this verse was revealed concerning so and so. They mean thereby that the conditions concerned by the verse include the condition of that particular event. This is as if they were presenting an illustration.

Examples of the above include verses revealed in the chapter *al-Barā'ah* concerning the hypocrites. These verses often start with the word ومنهم "and among them ..." That is why

1 Ibid., 292, ḥadīth no. 1816.

2 Muḥammad bin 'Abd Allāh al-Ḥākim,, *al-Mustadrak 'alā al-Ṣaḥīḥayn*, 2: 421, ḥadīth no. 3245. Al-Ḥākim declares it as meeting the standards of *al-Shaykhayn* and al-Dhahabī agrees with him at this point. See, ibid., footnote no. 3245.

‘Abd Allāh bin ‘Abbās said about this chapter: “we used to call it the chapter of condemnation.”[1]

Another example of this category is the verse: “It is never the wish of those without Faith among the People of the Book, nor of the Pagans, that anything good should come down to you from your Lord” (2:105). It goes without saying that this verse was revealed when some Jews started showing friendship toward the Muslims in Madīnah.

This is the category that is often mentioned by the narrators of events and some scholars of *tafsīr*. However, there is no use in mentioning it. And some of those with a narrow vision are misled by these occasions to confine the import of the verse to that particular event, since they fail to see the general import in its words.

(iv) Certain events have happened, and there are in the Qur’ān verses that convey a meaning fitting the event either prior to its occurrence or subsequent to it. And in the writings of some early scholars there appear expressions that give the impression that these events have been intended in these verses. Whereas their intention is only to say that these events fall within the scope of the meaning of the verse. The frequent difference of opinion among the Companions about the occasions of the revelation pertaining to this category also explains the nature of this category. This difference of opinion has been discussed in detail by al-Suyūṭī in the fifth issue in his work *al-Itqān*, in the light of numerous examples.[2]

Al-Suyūṭī also cites in his work a statement of al-Zarkashī to the effect that it is a well-known practice among the Companions and their successors that when any of them remarks about a verse that: “it has been revealed about such

1 Muḥammad bin Ismā‘īl al-Bukhārī, *Ṣaḥīḥ al-Bukhārī*, 865, ḥadīth no. 4882.

2 Jalāl al-Dīn ‘Abd al-Raḥmān al-Suyūṭī, *al-Itqān*, 1: 101-109.

and such ...", he only means that the verse contains that injunction, not that it has been revealed due to that.[1]

(v) That which explains brief statements and elaborates the meaning of figurative expressions. For instance, if someone thinks that in the verse "if any do fail to judge by (the light of) what Allah hath revealed, they are (no better than) unbelievers" (5:44), the preposition *man* is meant as a conditional clause, he will face a problem in understanding the verse. He will wonder how injustice in judgment could amount to disbelief. Then when he will find out that the occasion of the revelation concerned the Christians, he will know that the preposition *man* is subject-adjective. He will then understand that the purport of the verse is that those who left judging by *Injīl*, no wonder that they reject Prophet Muḥammad (peace be upon him).

Similar is the tradition of 'Abd Allāh bin Masʿūd. He says that when the verse "It is those who believe and confuse not their beliefs with wrong" (6:82), was revealed, it fell hard upon the Prophet's Companions who exclaimed: "which one of us does not adulterate his faith with injustice!" They were thinking that the word *ẓulm* occurring in the verse meant sin and wrongdoing. But the Prophet (peace be upon him) said: "it is not like that! Don't you hear Luqman's saying to his son: 'indeed *shirk* (ascribing partners with God), is a great injustice'."[2]

Also there is included in the occasions of the revelation a category that neither elaborates any brevity nor interprets a figurative statement. However, it enables us to understand the mutual links between different verses. For example, there is a verse in the chapter "Women": "If ye fear that ye shall not be able to deal justly with the orphans, marry women of your choice" (4:3); now it might be difficult to see the link

1 Ibid., 1: 101.

2 Muḥammad bin Ismā'īl al-Bukhārī, *Ṣaḥīḥ al-Bukhārī*, 839, ḥadīth no. 4776.

between to two parts of this conditional clause. This link has been explained by a tradition cited in *al-Ṣaḥīḥ* on the authority of 'Urwah bin al-Zubayr (may God be pleased with him). He had asked 'Ā'ishah (may God be pleased with her) about it. She replied as follows: "this is a reference to some orphan-girl who is under the care of her guardian and has a claim on his property. Her guardian wants to get married to her without being fair in paying her dowry. Such guardians have been forbidden from marrying those orphan-girls without fairly paying their dowries. At the same time, they were commanded to marry any women they liked other than those orphan-girls."

Further, the Qur'ān came as the Book of Guidance and legislation for the Ummah. This guidance may be provided before the need arises. Sometimes a group of people might be addressed by the Qur'ān for censure or approbation. At other times, all those people are addressed by it who are fit for its address. However, amidst all these addresses, it provides legislative and moral maxims and principles. The wisdom in all this is to make the understanding of religion by the *Ummah* easy, to make the teachings of Religion accessible by frequently reiterating them and to create among the scholars of the Ummah skills of deduction. For otherwise Allah was able to enlarge the volume of the Qur'ān manifold and to lengthen the lifetime of the Prophet (peace be upon him) more than those of Prophets Ibrāhīm and Mūsā (AS) so that he could go on laying down the laws under Divine mandate. That is why Allah Almighty declared unequivocally in the Qur'ān: "and I completed My favor upon you" (5:3). Therefore, just as it is forbidden to restrict the general words of the Qur'ān to any particular cases, because it nullifies the purport of Allah's speech, it is also wrong to generalize something that is meant for specifics and intended for restricted application. Because this will lead to distortion of meaning or even an outright abolition of the whole purport. Some sects had been misguided on account of this. Ibn Sīrīn says about the *Khawārij*: "they took the verses of warning addressed to the polytheists and applied them to the Muslims. The result of this misapplication was their heretic doctrine of declaring disbelief on account of sin."[1]

When some people said to 'Alī bin Abī Ṭālib (may God be pleased with him) on the day of arbitration, "None can command except Allah" (12:67), he remarked: "A true statement, but used for a wrong end!"[2] He also explained this remark in some of his sermons included in *Nahj al-Balāghah*.[3] There is also another great benefit of the occasions: as the Qur'ān is revealed when certain incidents occur, therein is an indication of its miraculous quality demonstrated by its spontaneous response to the incident. And the latter is one of the two well-known modes of eloquent speech of the Arab rhetoricians. Also its revelation on the occasion of certain events refutes the stance of those who claimed that the Qur'ān was a collection of early myths.

---

1 A similar view has been reported by Bukhārī in his Muḥammad bin Ismā'īl al-Bukhārī, *Ṣaḥīḥ al-Bukhārī*, ḥadīth no. 6929.

2 Muslim bin al-Ḥajjāj bin Muslim al-Qushayrī, *Ṣaḥīḥ Muslim*, 434, ḥadīth no. 2468.

3 'Alī bin Abī Ṭālib, *Nahj al-Balāghah*, Muḥammad al-Raḍī bin al-Ḥasan al-Mūsawī, comp., Muḥammad 'Abduhū, comm., Muḥammad Muḥy al-Dīn 'Abd al-Ḥamīd, ed. (n.p.: Maṭba'at al-Istiqāmah, n.d.), 1: 87.

CHAPTER SIX

OF RECITALS

We feel the need to include this subject of varied recitals because a majority of scholars have devoted special attention to this subject. Also, full-fledged works have been written by scholars of *tafsīr* to throw light on all the necessary aspects of the varied recitals of the Qur'ān. To enter into this discussion here despite the availability of these detailed works is justified only by the need to show its link with *tafsīr* and to appreciate the status of various recitals in terms of authenticity. This brief exposition here would explain my avoiding reference to many recitals during the course of this work.

I think there are two aspects to these varied recitals. One of these has nothing to do with *tafsīr*. While the other is related to it in many ways.

(i) The first aspect concerns the modes of speech that are exhibited through pronouncing letters and various punctuations, like long vowels, accents, light or heavy intonations, and other phonational or nasal variations. All these things have their origins in the linguistic varieties that existed in Arabic and were permitted by the Arab tradition at the time of the revelation. However, this variety has its basis in the Arabic language. Therefore, this aspect has not been included in any scholarly discussion of *tafsīr*, nor is it my intention here to do so if only because this aspect has no impact on determining the meaning of the Qur'ān.

When the masters of Arabic recited the Qur'ān, they did so in accordance with the dialects prevailing among the Arabs in their major civic centers where the scripts of the Qur'ān prepared by Sayyidunā 'Uthmān were distributed. These places were Madīnah, Makkah, Kūfā, Baṣra, Syria, and, according to some reports, Yemen and Baḥrayn. Reciters and experts in the Qur'ān from amongst the Companions were already living in these areas, before the copies of the master-script of 'Uthmān reached them. Each group living in these places recited the Qur'ān according to the mode of recital and pronunciation of his own people. However, this variety did not affect, increase or decrease in the letters. Nor did it affect the punctuation. In no way did these recitations differ from the master-script of 'Uthmān. It is possible that any reciter might have recited in two ways to show their correctness in Arabic language, in a bid to preserve Arabic language as the medium in which the Qur'ān was revealed. It is possible, therefore, that a great deal of this difference among reciters was intentional. This fact explains the criticism by al-Zamakhsharī and Ibn al-'Arabī of some modes of recital, though some of these criticisms also lend themselves to criticism.

Imām Mālik disliked, for example, reciting by slanting the long vowel (*imāla*) though it was established on the authority of the reciters. It has its basis in the report transmitted from Nāfi' the teacher of recitation at Madīnah on the authority of Warsh. This report has been exclusively relayed by the people of Egypt. The dislike by Imām Mālik shows that in his opinion this recitation was optional. There are other reports suggestive of variant readings. In my opinion, there is no harm in that so long as the words and phrases of the Qur'ān are preserved in the Book in the manner agreed to by all the Companions of the Prophet (peace be upon him) save a negligible few.

When 'Uthmān (may God be pleased with him) ordered the writing of the Book in accordance with the recitation of the

Prophet (peace be upon him) and the scribes of the Book authenticated it, he found it expedient to prescribe it as the authentic written version which should be followed by all the people. He collected all those copies that were contrary to this master-copy and burnt them. All the Companions agreed with his action. According to Shams al-Dīn al-Aṣfahānī, in part five of the introduction to his *tafsīr*: "'Alī used to recite the copy of 'Uthmān throughout his life and kept it as his authentic source."[1]

I think what 'Uthmān did was a completion of the task of collecting the Qur'ān initiated by Abū Bakr on the pattern of the Prophet's recital. 'Uthmān prepared several copies for distribution in the major cities. Thus almost a consensus was established on the authenticity of 'Uthmān's copy and the recital according to it. By the same token all other versions were rejected. This is why the scholars of recitations and the jurists of Islam have agreed that a) any reading that conforms to a valid mode in Arabic language, b) conforms to the script of 'Uthmān's copy and c) and is established by a correct chain of narrators shall be considered authentic, not liable to rejection.

The above three conditions however, do not equate the modes of recital, thus proved, with the version that has reached the highest degree of authenticity (*tawātur*). These modes, when they fulfill the conditions, shall be equal to something attributed to the Prophet through a correct chain of narrators. These modes that have been found fulfilling the three conditions are ten in number, attributed to ten masters of recitation. These ten are acknowledged as the authentic modes of reciting the Qur'ān.

---

1 Abū Muḥammad Ḥusayn al-Baghawī, *Sharḥ al-Sunnah*, Shu'ayb al-Arna'ūṭ and Zuhayr al-Shāwesh (eds.) (Beirut: al-Maktab al-Islāmī, 1403 AH), 4/525.

(ii) The second aspect of difference in recitals is that which occurs between the reciters in the letter of words like: *Māliki Yawm al-Dīn and Maliki Yawm al-Dīn*, *nanshuruhā* and *nunshizuhā*, *waẓannū annahum qad kudhdhibū* (with an accented *dhāl*) and *qad kudhibū* (without accent on *dhāl*). It also includes such difference in the punctuation that brings a change in the meaning of a verb. For example the verse:

"When (Jesus) the son of Mary is held up as an example,
behold, thy people raise a clamour thereat
(in ridicule)!" (43:57).

In this verse, Nāfi' recited *Yaṣuddūn* while Ḥamza recited *Yaṣiddūn*. The first version gives a transitive meaning: 'preventing others from belief' and the second version gives an intransitive sense: "they refrain from believing". The context of the verse provides room for both the meanings.

This latter aspect of the difference in recitation does have a close link with *tafsīr*. This is because proving one word in a version might explain the meaning of its counterpart in the other version. Or it may suggest another meaning. Knowledge of this variety in recital is also significant for *tafsīr* because this variance enriches the meanings of a verse. Examples of these variations are: (*Ḥatta Yaṭṭahharna*) and (*Ḥatta Yaṭhurna*), and (*Lāmastum al-Nisā'*), and (*lamastum al-Nisā'*). The probability is that revelation has been both ways and even more to invest it with abundant meaning. This is premised on the firm stand that all varied readings are rightly attributed to the Prophet (peace be upon him). Also it is included in the probability that the words coming from Allah Almighty admitted all these versions intentionally to enrich their meanings. The presence of two or more modes of recitations would then counterweigh two or more verses. This can be compared to *taḍmīn* in the Arabic language, *tawriyah* or *tawjīh* in the stylistics (*al-Badī'*) and the auxiliary constructions in Rhetoric (*Ma'āni*). In this way, it displays the conformity of the Qur'ān to the rhetorical (بلاغة) standards. That is why the difference among the reciters could result in the difference in meaning as well where one mode of recital was not definitely preferable to the other. Though we find that the words of Abū 'Alī al-Fārisī in his work on the subject entitled *al-Ḥujjah* imply that he favored preferring the meaning of one recital over the other.[1] In my opinion, however, it is the duty of the *mufassir* to explain the variation of readings because it affords abundance in meaning quite often. In this way, I see the variety of recitals at par with the variety of the Qur'ānic words.

The authentic basis for the variant readings is provided by a tradition of 'Umar (may God be pleased with him) reported by Bukhārī in which the Prophet (peace be upon him) affirmed two different modes of reciting by 'Umar (may God be pleased with him) and Hishām bin Ḥakīm bin Ḥizām. The former had found the latter reciting part of the chapter "Poets" (*al-Shu'arā'*) differently from his own way. He objected to it and both of them referred their dispute to the Prophet (peace be upon him). The Prophet (peace be upon him) affirmed both modes of recital and said: "so it has been revealed. Indeed this Qur'ān has been revealed with seven modes (*Sab'at Aḥruf*). You may recite the one which is convenient!"[2]

However, this tradition is problematic. The scholars have held different views about it. These views emanate from two considerations: (i) considering this tradition as abrogated; and (ii) considering it as valid and sound (*Muḥkam*).

Those who consider it abrogated is a group of scholars that includes Abū Bakr al-Bāqillānī, Ibn 'Abd al-Barr, Abū Bakr bin al-'Arabī, al-Ṭabarī and al-Ṭaḥāwī.[3] The same view is also attributed to Sufyān bin 'Uyaynah and Ibn Wahb.[4] They say that this was an allowance

1 See, Abū 'Alī al-Ḥasan bin 'Abd al-Ghaffār al-Fārisī, *al-Ḥujjah li al-Qurrā' al-Sab'ah*, Badr al-Dīn Qahwajī and Bashīr Juwayjātī, eds. (Damascus & Beirut: Dār al-Ma'mūn li al-Turāth, 1404/1984-1419/1999), 7 vols.

2 Muḥammad bin Ismā'īl al-Bukhārī, *Ṣaḥīḥ al-Bukhārī*, 389, ḥadīth no. 2419.

3 Jalāl al-Dīn 'Abd al-Raḥmān al-Suyūṭī, *al-Itqān*, 1: 148-49.

4 Ibid., 1: 148.

(*Rukhsah*) granted in the beginning of Islam. Allah had permitted the Arabs to read the Qur'ān in their own dialects, to which they were accustomed. Then this permission was abrogated by prescribing the standard of the Quraysh in the language because the Qur'ān was revealed in their language. And this prescription was for all the people. Also due to excessive memorizing and scribing of the Qur'ān, the excuse for that allowance was no longer valid.[1] Ibn Al-'Arabī says that this allowance was valid only during the Prophet's lifetime and after his demise it was abrogated. This abrogation was either based on the consensus of the Companions or on the will of the Prophet (peace be upon him).[2] Their argument in favor of this view is the statement of 'Umar (may God be pleased with him) "the Qur'ān was revealed in the language of the Quraysh."[3]

They also rely for their view on the direction of 'Uthmān (may God be pleased with him) to the scribes of the Qur'ān to the effect that in case of difference among them over a word, they should write it in the language of the Quraysh, since the Qur'ān was revealed in their language.[4] What he meant was that the predominant language of the Qur'ān was that of the Quraysh. Or he meant that it was revealed in the language that they spoke or which dominated their language among the languages of tribes. This was because the cultural event of *'Ukāẓ* used to be held in the land of the Quraysh and Makkah was the place that attracted all the tribes. Therefore, the language of the Quraysh combined the common features of all linguistic variety of Arab tribes.

As to the permission being limited to seven paroles, scholars have put forward several explanations for that; however, in our view, the

---

1 Ibid., 1: 149.

2 See, Abū Bakr bin al-'Arabī, *'Āriḍat al-Aḥwadhī*, Ṣidqī Jamīl al-'Aṭṭār, ed. (Beirut: Dār al-Fikr li al-Ṭibā'ah wa al-Nashr wa al-Tawzī', 1425-26/2005), 6: 63-64; idem., *Aḥkām al-Qur'ān*, 'Alī Muḥammad al-Bajāwī, ed. (Beirut: Dār al-Ma'rifah li al-Ṭibā'ah wa al-Nashr, n.d.), 2: 1039-40, 4: 1691-92; idem., *Kitāb al-'Awāṣim min al-Qawāṣim*, 2: 193 ff.

3 Aḥmad bin 'Alī bin Ḥajar al-'Asqalānī, *Fatḥ al-Bārī Sharḥ Ṣaḥīḥ al-Bukhārī* (Riyadh: Dār al-Salām, 1418/1998), 9: 13.

4 Muḥammad bin Ismā'īl al-Bukhārī, *Ṣaḥīḥ al-Bukhārī*, 589, ḥadīth no. 3506.

following appears to be the best: the meaning of 'paroles' is those dialects of Arabs such as: straightened vowel and slanted vowel, stretched and short voice, pronouncing *hamzah* and dropping it. Subject to preserving the words of the Qur'ān, Arabs were permitted to use these varieties of dialect. There are a number of other explanations also, but they are not worthy of notice by the scholars. I believe that the reported difference between 'Umar (may God be pleased with him) and Hishām (may God be pleased with him) can be explained in the following way: that Hishām (may God be pleased with him) might have read the chapter al-Furqān in a different order of verses than 'Umar (may God be pleased with him). The Prophet (peace be upon him) might have permitted them to memorize the chapters of the Qur'ān without observing the order of the verses. Al-Bāqillānī has expressed the possibility that the order between chapters might have been devised by the Companions through their *ijtihād* as we shall explain in the eighth part of this introduction.[1] Therefore, in our view, this might have been a temporary permission. Thereafter, however, people went on following the pattern of the Prophet (peace be upon him) in the recitation of the Qur'ān which was compiled by Abū Bakr (may God be pleased with him) in accordance with the last public recital of the Prophet (peace be upon him). Thus at the time of Abū Bakr (may God be pleased with him), the Companions reached a consensus on the compiled copy of the Qur'ān, because they were aware that the cause of special permission was no more applicable.

Some people suppose that the number of seven refers to those seven styles of reciting that are famous among the reciters. This is wrong and no scholar of the Qur'ān has ever maintained it.

As to the condition that for a reading to be acceptable, it must be supported by an authentic chain of transmitters, this is an essential

---

1 Abū Bakr bin al-Ṭayyib al-Bāqillānī, *al-Intiṣār li al-Qur'ān*, Muḥammad 'Iṣām al-Quḍāt, ed. (Amman & Beirut: Dār al-Fatḥ li al-Nashr wa al-Tawzī' & Dār Ibn Ḥazm li al-Ṭibā'ah wa al-Nashr wa al-Tawzī', 1422/2001), 1: 279.

condition no doubt. There could be some reading conforming to both the script of 'Uthmān (may God be pleased with him) as well as the rules of Arabic, yet it will not be permitted for want of authentic reporting. For example, as reported about Ḥammād bin al-Zabarqān in *Al-Muzhir* that he read: "only because of a promise he had made to him" (9:114) by *bā'* in the last word instead of *yā'* as in the established reading. Now despite its being present in 'Uthmān's script as well as its correctness in the grammar, it will not be acceptable due to lack of authenticity.

According to Abu Bakr bin al-'Arabī, in *al-'Awāṣim*, the consensus of scholars is that all forms of recital that conform to the standard script of 'Uthmān are established as *mutawātir* even if these differ in their pronunciation and phonetics. This status of authenticity is, however, contingent upon the general publicity of their reports that must be attributed to at least two Companions. Then their prevalence among the community and the tacit approval by the majority of knowledgeable men of different generations lends further credibility to these readings. The fundamental condition, nevertheless, remains their strict conformity to the master script of 'Uthmān (may God be pleased with him).[1]

The reports of the ten most famous forms of recital are attributed to the following eight prominent Companions of the Prophet (peace be upon him): 'Umar bin al-Khaṭṭāb (may God be pleased with him), 'Uthmān bin ʿAffān (may God be pleased with him), 'Alī bin Abī Ṭālib (may God be pleased with him), 'Abd Allāh bin Masʿūd (may God be pleased with him), Ubayy bin Ka'b (may God be pleased with him), Abū al-Dardā' (may God be pleased with him), Zayd bin Thābit (may God be pleased with him) and Abū Mūsā al-Ashʿarī (may God be pleased with him). Some of the reports are traced to all the above eight while others reach some of them.

As to the punctuation, characters and accents in the Qur'ān, they are mostly established by the highest credible authenticity (*tawātur*). There

1 Al-Qāḍī Abū Bakr bin al-'Arabī, *Kitāb al-'Awāsim min al-Qawāsim*, 2: 193 ff.

are minor exceptions, however, to the unified system. But these differences are negligible in number and do not affect the connotation of the text. There are certain other differences claimed by some sects in order to find support from the Qur'ān in favor of their peculiar doctrines. For example, some of the *Mu'tazila* have recited the verse: "and to Moses Allah spoke directly" (4:164) by converting the word Allah from its status as subject in the sentence to an object.[1] This they have done because they wanted thereby to deny the attribute of speech to Allah (peace be upon him).

The scholars have also discussed the possibility of preference between these established forms of recital. Most of them hold that it is permissible to take a preference. These include Imām Muḥammad bin Jarīr al-Ṭabarī and al-'Allāmah al-Zamakhsharī. When Ibn Rushd was asked about it, he also answered in the affirmative adding that the report of 'Warsh' was preferred in his own country, Spain.[2]

If preference is possible and permitted between variant recitals, then the question arises whether there is any difference between these recitals from the miraculous aspects of the Qur'ān?

We think that miracle in the Qur'ān is defined as: 'conformity of speech to the requirement of the condition'. In this respect, there could be no difference between various readings of the Qur'ān. However, it is possible that some of the miraculous speech might contain subtleties and stylistic features like alliteration and exaggeration or greater eloquence or particular figures of speech. It is possible that one form of recital might be more prominent in this respect than others; also because some of these were permitted by the Prophet (peace be upon him) for the sake of convenience as already noted in the report about 'Umar and Hishām (may God be pleased with him).

---

1 Maḥmūd bin 'Umar al-Zamakhsharī, *al-Kashshāf*, 2: 179.

2 See, Abū al-Walīd bin Rush al-Andalusī, *al-Bayān wa al-Taḥṣīl wa al-Sharḥ wa al-Tawjīh wa al-Ta'līl fī Masā'il al-Mustakhrajah*, Muḥammad Ḥajjī, ed., 2nd ed. (Beirut: Dār al-Gharb al-Islāmī, 1408/1988), 1: 358.

CHAPTER SEVEN

STORIES OF THE QUR'ĀN

Allah Almighty has stated in the Qur'ān:

"We do relate unto thee the most beautiful of stories, in that We reveal to thee this (portion of the) Qur'ān: before this, thou too was among those who knew it not" (12:3)

that the narration of past stories in this Book are a favor to the Prophet (peace be upon him). The word (*aḥsan*) "best" in the above verse shows that the stories in the Qur'ān are not designed to amuse or entertain the listeners, nor are these anecdotes intended to bewilder the audience by whatever element of good or evil they contain. Because the aim of the Qur'ān is higher and nobler than these. For, if it were not so, then these stories would have been just like any other stories. There would have been no distinction attached to them.

A story (*qiṣṣa*) is a report about an incident removed from the one who is being informed about it. That is why there are no stories in the Qur'ān about the encounter of the Muslims with their enemies at the time of its revelation.

The plural of *qiṣṣa* is *qiṣaṣ*. The word *qaṣaṣ* is a noun indicating the related story. It is an infinitive that carries the sense of an object (*maf'ūl*). When someone uses it as a verb *qaṣṣa*, it gives the sense of relating a news or story.

The scholars have been alive to the fact that the purpose of relating these stories is not restricted to deriving lessons or to preaching from whatever good or evil these stories contain. Nor do these stories merely aim at extolling some of their actors and condemning others, as some superficial people have supposed. But their aim is higher and nobler.

These stories are replete with morals and benefits for the Ummah. That is why we find the Qur'ān taking from every story its noblest aspect and leaving the rest, so that its treatment of these stories could prevent any intention of seeking an amusement from them.

That is why these stories were not mentioned continuously in the Qur'ān in one or more chapters like the common books of history. Rather these stories were distributed in parts over places suitable for them. Because the benefits accruing from them have a link with this distribution. Since these stories are meant to be a remembrance and counsel for men of religion, these are more similar to oration. The Qur'ān has a peculiar style in presenting these themes that is reflected in the verses dealing with them. This style is at once that of remembering and reminding. It is by far nobler than the style of storytellers who narrate stories for their own sake. Whereas the Qur'ān brings up its stories at their proper places to give them a dual character: argument and elaboration. We also find that a distinctive feature of the Qur'ānic stories is following a mode of conciseness. This conciseness underlines the moral purpose of the story rather than mere narration.

Another distinction is that the Qur'ān omits those details that are a natural consequence of the narration. For example, in the chapter Yūsuf, it says: "So they both raced each other to the door" (12:25) omitting mention of the coming of her husband, his knocking the door and their rushing to open it. Yūsuf rushed to prevent the lady from her intention to show her husband that he had intended evil against her. While the lady rushed to the door to be the first to present the case before him and prevent Yūsuf from reaching him before her. All this was later indicated by the following words: "they both found her lord near the door. She said: 'What is the (fitting) punishment for one who formed an evil design against thy wife, but prison or a grievous chastisement'" (12:25).

Another feature of the Qur'ānic stories is that these are presented in a majestic style to emphasize the wise counsel contained in them. At the same time, the Qur'ān maintains observance of the real objective of legislation and warning. All these features deliver the following ten benefits.

i. The height of knowledge possessed by the "people of the book" in that age was an awareness about the stories of the Prophets and their strife, along with the conditions of their neighboring communities. To reveal these stories that were known exclusively by men of profound knowledge among the "people of the book" was a great challenge for them. This rendered them without argument against Muslims. The Qur'ān said: "Such are some of the stories of the unseen, which We have revealed unto thee: before this, neither thou nor thy people knew them" (11:49).

   Thus, those who possessed knowledge of the Qur'ān were more worthy of having the knowledge that had been a preserve of the Jewish priests. In this way, the stigma of lacking knowledge was removed from the Muslims in the eyes of the Jews.

ii. The tradition of *sharī'ah* includes knowledge of the past history of similar prescriptions revealed to earlier Prophets. Mentioning the stories of these Prophets and their peoples by the Qur'ān exalted the status of Islamic *sharī'ah* with the mention of the history of legislators. The Qur'ān says: "How many of the prophets fought (in Allah's way), and with them (fought) large bands of godly men?" (3:146).

   In the same continuity with the past we are also at present reaping the benefits of this age-old struggle of the Prophets who went before. I have noticed that the Qur'ānic style of narrating such stories only speaks of the strength or weakness of faith of the individual actors in the story, and does not go beyond this focus. It only brings out the Divine approval or condemnation that comes in the wake of these stories. In this style, you will not find any mention of habitats or genealogy, since the real importance is attached to the belief of a past people, or their unbelief. For example, we find in the narration of the story of the people of the cave, the focus is on taking morals from the supreme power of Allah shown in this story. That is why the Qur'ān makes no mention of their ethnic origin or their particular era. Because the whole lesson to be learnt in the story is from their miraculous manner of resurrection and the reaching of their emissary into the city thereafter.

iii. Highlighting the benefit of knowing past history in terms of cause and effect that bring up good and evil, construction and destruction so that the Ummah could take lessons and observe caution in its present conduct. At the same time, these narrations also underline the ultimate triumph of the higher values of life and of the nobility of human character.

iv. A lesson to the non-Muslims, especially the polytheists, from the fate of the people who opposed their prophets and disobeyed the command of their Lord, so that they refrain from their mischief by learning from the examples of their counterparts. They could also register the fact that real victory on earth eventually returns to the virtuous people. The Qur'ān declares: "So relate the story; perchance they may reflect" (7:176), and it says: "There is, in their stories, instruction for men endued with understanding" (12:111), and it says: "Before this We wrote in the Psalms, after the Message (given to Moses): My servants the righteous, shall inherit the earth" (21:105).

All these facts of history are reiterated in these stories in which are mentioned those who denied the Prophets like stories of the peoples of Nūḥ, 'Ād, Thamūd, the people of Rass, and the inhabitants of Aykah.

v. In the narration of these stories, there is a style of description and dialogue. This style was not familiar to the Arabs. Its mention in the Qur'ān was the introduction of a new style in the Arabic Rhetoric, a style that had a great impact on the minds of the Arabs. And indeed this style is among the miraculous traits of the Qur'ān. The Arabs could not deny the wonderful innovation in this style that was inimitable to them. For example, see the narration of the conditions of people in the Paradise and Hell and the "people of the heights" in the chapter "Heights". This style was a feature of the Qur'ān that further convinced the Arabs that they were unable to emulate the Qur'ān, acknowledging its inimitable character.

vi. Due to their immersion in long ignorance and lack of knowledge, the Arabs were not prone to comprehending things beyond sense-perception. Whatever lay outside this narrow cognitive scope escaped their imagination and grasp. Hence they lacked the benefit of taking lessons from the experience of past nations of which they had little knowledge. Even those nations with whose names they were familiar, they did know about their antecedents. This ignorance led to lack of concern for reforming their own lot and guarding against the ills that had brought about downfall of those before them.

The narration of past stories by the Qur'ān expanded the knowledge of Muslims about plurality of nations and their capricious conditions. Referring to this ignorance of the Arabs before Islam, the Qur'ān says: "And ye dwelt in the dwellings of men who wronged their own souls; ye were clearly shown how We dealt with them" (14:45).

vii. To familiarize the Muslims with the expanses of the world and greatness of nations while acknowledging their distinctive traits so that they could overcome their arrogance. This arrogance was typically mentioned with reference to the people 'Ād who asserted: "and said: 'Who is superior to us in strength?'" (41:15). When a community learns of the distinct qualities of other nations and becomes familiar with the life patterns of others, it seeks those things that it lacks in order to reform and improve its own life.

viii. To create among Muslims a drive to lead the world like previous people before them did and to bring them out of their stagnation. The Arabs were in those days merely satisfied by mutual killing and plunder. Their ambitions were exhausted by such narrow ambitions. They were unable to seek or aspire for any leadership of significance in the world. They lived in this state of mind until they lost all honor and prestige. They became almost subservient to the Persian or Roman powers of their time. The whole of Iraq, Yemen and Bahrayn were subservient to the political power of the Persians. While Syria and its adjacent areas were loyal to the Romans. The remaining areas of Hijāz and Najd had no option but to seek honor from the local kings and potentates of Persians and Romans in their trades and travels.

ix. Creating awareness that Allah's power is above all worldly powers. It is He who helps whomsoever He wills. And that if they adopted the two means of survival: preparation and confidence, they could remain immune from the domination of others. For this purpose, the Qur'ān mentioned the good consequences of the virtuous people and the nature of Divine support for them. As He told them, for example, in this verse: "But he cried through the depth of darkness, "There is no god but thou: glory to thee: I was indeed wrong!". So We listened to him: and delivered him from distress: and thus do We deliver those who have faith" (21:87-88).

x. The indirect advantages that were obtained through awareness about history of law and civilization by opening the minds of the Muslims to the benefits of civilization.

The above discussion will hopefully have dispelled doubts in some minds about the repeated mention of the same story in the Qur'ān. Many people of varying levels of understanding, for different reasons, wonder why one story was not considered sufficient to achieve the required aim? And further why the same story was repeatedly mentioned? To answer all such wondering minds, we would say that the Qur'ān is more a sermon and an oration than a compiled book. Therefore, the benefits of the story are mentioned by the requirement of the context and occasion. The story, or a part of it, is cited as a sort of argument to substantiate a contention. Hence its mention elsewhere is not a repetition because its earlier mention was in a different context. It is like an orator who cites the same thing in a subsequent speech because the situation so demands. He should not be considered repetitive on account of this.

Besides, there are also other benefits to the frequent mention of the same story by the Qur'ān.

(1) It helps to instill its lessons in the mind.

(2) It displays the rhetorical quality of the Qur'ān, because repeating the same phrase on one subject is cumbersome for an eloquent orator. But when the subsequent mention is done by a varied mode of communication, employing metaphors and figurations and new words and construction of words and synonyms and various verbal ornamentations are introduced through different figures of speech. All these things greatly augment the rhetorical quality of the Qur'ān, which shows itself to its audience more closely.

(3) The new converts among Muslims could hear those stories that they missed earlier before they had embraced the faith. For reception of the Qur'ān at the time of its revelation is far more impactful in the mind than receiving it from memories of people.

(4) All Muslims did not collect the whole of the Qur'ān at the time of its revelation. Some people learnt some chapters with certain

stories in it. At the same time, others learnt other chapters in which the stories were mentioned in part or in whole.

(5) These stories are mentioned in different styles. In a mention of the same story at two or more places, different styles have been adopted depending on the requirements of different contexts.

Also what is sometimes mentioned in one place is not mentioned in other places for the following reasons: to avoid lengthy narration of the same story and to focus only on the moral of the story. In another place, some other point is focused by the demand of the occasion. Thus, in the whole Qur'ān, a complete story is obtained and its purpose is achieved in its entirety. Also at some place is found an explanation for the story that is briefly mentioned in another place. Similarly, in places, a part of the story that is suitable for the listeners is mentioned in one place while another part is mentioned elsewhere for the same reason. Because a story is sometimes brought to bear upon the conditions of the Polytheists, or Jews and Christians or Believers or both. At times, a story is related to all these groups at once, in a certain state. Then it is related elsewhere in another way. For all the above occasions the speech will differ in terms of brevity and elaborateness. For example, the story of Prophet Mūsā has been elaborately mentioned in the chapter "*Ṭāhā*" and the chapter "Poets". But the same story was compressed in the following two verses in the chapter *al-Furqān*:

(Before this,) We sent to Moses The Book, and appointed his brother Aaron with him as minister. And We commanded: "Go ye both, to the people who have rejected our Signs:" And those (people) We destroyed with utter destruction (25:35-36).

At other times, some mistake held about a certain story is corrected and at others it is not intended.

These are the findings that I could reach on the subject. Some of these thoughts might have been found less clearly in the previous works.

CHAPTER EIGHT

THE NAMES OF THE QUR'ĀN, ITS CHAPTERS, THEIR ORDER AND NAMES

This is a subject that has a strong link with both the Qur'ān and its *tafsīr*. Because what will be cleared here is of benefit in appreciating many openings of the chapters of the Qur'ān, and their mutual relations.

It is already known that the subject matter of *tafsīr* is the explanation of the Qur'ān and the guidance, and the modes and etiquettes of reforming the Ummah internally and externally, that this Book contains. And this is attained by comprehending the linguistic and rhetorical significations of the Qur'ān. The Qur'ān is the Speech revealed in the Arabic language by Allah to Muḥammad (peace be upon him) through Jibrīl. The Prophet (peace be upon him) was in turn charged with the duty of conveying it to the *Ummah* in the same words in which it was revealed to him, so that they could act upon it and recite it in their prayers and as a form of worship according to their convenience.

Allah also made the Qur'ān a sign of the truth of the Prophet's claim to carry the message from Allah for the whole of mankind. This was done by challenging its opponents and skeptics among the Arabs in a manner that they could not oppose it. Because when the Qur'ān invited them to take up this challenge, they failed to do so. First, they were asked to bring ten chapters similar to it (11:13); then the challenge was softened and they were asked to produce one chapter like it (10:38). Thereafter, the Qur'ān clearly proclaimed their failure and declared that they shall never be able to meet this challenge (2:24).

Thus the Qur'ān is the name of the Speech revealed to the Prophet (peace be upon him) as written in totality in the scriptures containing one hundred fourteen chapters starting from the chapter "The Opening" and ending in the chapter "The People". The word Qur'ān has become the proper name of the Book.[1] It takes the form of *fu'lān* like *ghufrān* and *shukrān*. We find many proper names in Arabic containing *nūn* like 'Uthmān, Ḥassān, and 'Adnān. The overwhelming view about the etymological explanation of the word Qur'ān is that it is so named because it is recited and further because its very first verses were revealed to command recitation.

Thus the word Qur'ān is the proper name given to the Revelation sent to Prophet Muḥammad (peace be upon him). It is the most famous of its names. And this name was never given to any other Book. Also this is the name more often mentioned in the verses of the Qur'ān itself and was used in the language of the early scholars of Islam.

Apart from this, the Qur'ān has other names that are adjectival or generic in origin. The author of *al-Itqān* has counted more than twenty such names.[2] The most famous of these are: *Tanzīl*, *Kitāb*, *Furqān*, *Dhikr*, *Waḥy* and *Kalām Allāh*.

As to *Furqān*, it is in fact an infinitive noun that means something which discriminates between right and wrong. That is why the day of *Badr* was called the "day of *Furqān*".[3] This word has also been used as adjective for the Qur'ān in the verse "Blessed is He who sent down the criterion to His servant" (25:1).

It has been so called because it is distinct from earlier scriptures in its function of distinguishing between truth and falsehood. The Qur'ān always supports its guidance with arguments and precedents. It is enough to cite the elaborate description of *tawḥīd* and Divine Attributes found in the Qur'ān, something that is nowhere seen in *Tawrāh* (Torah) or *Injīl* (Gospels). For example, the Qur'ān says: "there is nothing whatever like unto Him" (42:11).

---

1 Jalāl al-Dīn 'Abd al-Raḥmān al-Suyūṭī, *al-Itqān*, 1: 161-62.

2 Jalāl al-Dīn 'Abd al-Raḥmān al-Suyūṭī, *al-Itqān*, 1: 159-61.

3 Muḥammad bin Jarīr al-Ṭabarī, *Jāmi' al-Bayān 'an Ta'wīl Āyy al-Qur'ān*, 1: 110.

Further, apart from the fact that the Qur'ān presents itself as the 'criterion' that distinguishes between right and wrong, it also emphasizes in many verses its status as a "protector" of earlier scriptures such as *Tawrāh* and *Injīl* in that the former has preserved in its fold the essence of the latter's message.

All this meaning is included in the term Qur'ān being the Book that pervades and protects all previous scriptures as it says about itself "To thee We sent the Scripture in truth, confirming the scripture that came before it, and guarding it in safety" (5:48).

A statement of this predominant feature of the Qur'ān is also found in the beginning of the chapter "Āl 'Imrān".

The word *Tanzīl* is an infinitive noun derived from the verb: *nazzala*. The Qur'ān has been so named because its words have been sent down piecemeal from the heavens in installments. Allah says: "A Revelation from (Allah), Most Gracious, Most Merciful. A Book, whereof the verses are explained in detail; a Qur'an in Arabic, for people who understand" (41:2-3), and "(This is) the Revelation of the Book in which there is no doubt, from the Lord of the Worlds" (32:2).

And the word *Kitāb* is a generic name assumed to often refer to the Qur'ān. The Qur'ān says "This is the Book without doubt" (2:2); and it says "Praise be to Allah, Who hath sent to His Servant the Book" (18:1).

It has been named *al-Kitāb* (The Book) because Allah Almighty has made it an all-inclusive compendium of the *sharī'ah*. Thus it is like *Tawrāh* which was written at the time of the Messenger who was sent with it. And it is similar to *Injīl* which was not written at the time of the Messenger who was sent with it, but was written down later by some of his followers. And it is called "The Book" because Allah has commanded His Messenger to arrange the writing down of whatever was revealed to him so that it served as evidence for those who entered Islam subsequently and might have not learnt it by heart. In giving it this name, there is a miracle of the Prophet (peace be upon him) which shows itself in the fact that what was revealed to him was going to be written in the scripts. Therefore, the Prophet chose scribes from amongst his Companions to write down what was revealed to him. When finally Abū Bakr al-Ṣiddīq *ordered the writing of the Scripture, it was already preserved by the Muslims in their hearts.*

Another word is *al-Dhikr* (The Remembrance/The Counsel) as the Qur'ān says: "and We have sent down unto thee (also) the Message that thou mayest explain clearly to men what is sent for them" (16:44). Thus it is a reminder to people of their obligations in belief and action.

Another word is *al-Waḥy* as mentioned in this verse "Say, I do but warn you according to Revelation" (21:45). The reason for this name is that the Qur'ān was revealed to the Prophet (peace be upon him) through the Angel and such a communication through the Angel is called *Waḥy*. Since it represents the will of Allah, it is like a speech that represents the intent of man, even though the construction of its words is not a human act.

Another word used for the Book is the Speech of God (*Kalām Allāh*) in the verse: "If one amongst the Pagans ask thee for asylum, grant it to him, so that he may hear the word of Allah" (9:6).

It should be known that when Abū Bakr al-Ṣiddīq (may God be pleased with him) commissioned the collection and writing of the Qur'ān, it was written down on the paper. He asked the Companions to suggest a name for it. Some of them suggested *Injīl*, but this was rejected because of its association with the Christians. Some others suggested *Sifr*. This was also disapproved if because the Jews called the *Tawrāh "Asfār"* (the plural of *sifr*). At this point 'Abd Allāh bin Mas'ūd said: 'I have seen a script in Abyssinia which they called: *muṣḥaf*. So they named it *al-Muṣḥaf*.[1]

---

1 Jalāl al-Dīn 'Abd al-Raḥmān al-Suyūṭī, *al-Itqān*, 1: 164.

8.1. Verses of the Qur'ān

Āyah is a composite unit of the Qur'ān. Its being composite might be a "presumed" or "subsequent construction". I have added the word "presumed" to include (*Mudhāmmatān*) "Dark-green in color (from plentiful watering)" (55:27) because it is presumably *Mudhāmmatān*. Another example of a presumed composite is *wa al-Fajr* "By the break of Day" (89:1) which is regarded a verse on the presumption that it is actually "I swear by the dawn". And I have added the word "subsequent" because some openings of chapters from the "disjointed letters" (*al-ḥurūf al-muqaṭṭa'ah*) should be included since these are mostly treated as verses in the scripture, excluding *Alif Lām Rā*, *Alif Lām Mīm Rā* and *Ṭā Sīn*.

This is an issue settled on the basis of the Prophet's pronouncing of his authority on the subject and has been a consistently followed practice. There is, therefore, no difference between these and others. Naming these units of the Book verses (*āyāt*) is an innovation of the Qur'ān. The Qur'ān says: "He it is Who has sent down to thee the Book: In it are verses basic or fundamental (of established meaning)" (3:7) and it says elsewhere: "(This is) a Book, with verses basic or fundamental (of established meaning), further explained in detail" (11:1). This has been named *āyah* (sign) because a verse is an evidence of its being a revelation from Allah to the Prophet (peace be upon him). It is an evidence in that it contains within its fold the highest degree of rhetorical perfection in the symmetry of the speech. Also its coming together with other *āyāt* is evidence that the Qur'ān has been revealed from Allah and it has not been authored by a human. Because the Prophet (peace be upon him) presented it as a challenge to men of eloquence and elegant speech, but they failed to produce even a single chapter similar to it.

That is why the sentences of *Injīl* and *Tawrāh* could not be called verses: because the Hebrew and Aramaic languages do not have those singular stylistic qualities that characterize the Arabic verses of the Qur'ān.

The measure of Qur'ānic verses has been determined by the Prophet (peace be upon him). In several verses, though, traditions may differ. This shows flexibility in determining the beginning and end of some verses. However, the Companions of the Prophet (peace be upon him) were well aware of the limits of the verses.

At the time of the Prophet (peace be upon him) and after, the Muslims used to assess duration of time by the measure of what a reciter could recite in this time-span. For example, it has been said that the duration between the Prophet's pre-dawn meal in Ramaḍan and the break of dawn was equivalent to the recitation of fifty verses.

Abū Bakr bin al-'Arabī says "the determining of the verses is a formidable task in the Qur'ān; because some verses are short and others long. Some break in the middle of speech while others complete it."[1] Al-Zamakhsharī *says: "the matter of verses is a knowledge derived from traditional authority and it is not something which is subject to opinion."*[2] I think it probable that the volume of a verse was determined upon the completion of its revelation which was indicated by the terminal pause *(fāṣilah)*.

I also think that these terminal pauses are those words the ending letters of which are similar or proximate and these letters are also phonetically allied or akin to each other. And these terminal pauses are repeated in the chapter so much that these seem to be intended in the symmetrical scheme running through several similar verses. These verses could be few or many. Many of them are similar to the rhymed speech.

The criteria in these kinds of verses are the similar constructions of words in punctuation and they are more like the rhymes of poetry that are observed for the sake of maintaining the rhymes.

1 Jalāl al-Dīn 'Abd al-Raḥmān al-Suyūṭī, *al-Itqān fī 'Ulūm al-Qur'ān*, Muḥammad Abū al-Faḍl Ibrāhīm, ed. (Cairo: al-Hay'ah al-Miṣriyyah al-'Āmmah li al-Kitāb, 1974), 1: 231 (Ed.)

2 Maḥmūd bin 'Umar al-Zamakhsharī, *al-Kashshāf*, 1: 140.

I have observed that all these terminal pauses are also the endings of verses even if the speech wherein these occur, does not complete the purport of communication.

It should be borne in mind that these terminal pauses in rhymed constructions provide an added miraculous quality to the Qur'ān *because these greatly ornament the speech. The minds of the listeners register the impact of their similar endings with remarkable phonetic affinity like the rhythms of poetry or rhymes of prose.* That is why it is appropriate to pause over these endings of verses in order to bring out their phonetic beauty. Many traditions support this. For example, al-Bayhaqī reports in *Shu'ab al-Īmān*, as it has been mentioned by al-Suyūṭī, the view that "it is better to stop at these endings of verses even though these were linked with onward speech in order to emulate the Prophet's example."[1] Abū Dāwūd reports in his Sunan on the authority of Umm Salamah who said: "the Prophet (peace be upon him), when he recited the Qur'ān, used to recite in pieces and would stop at each ending."[2]

These reports suggest that tradition must be followed to determine the limits of verses, as stated by Ibn al-'Arabī and Zamakhsharī. However, this should not deter us from the efforts to lay down rules to guide the readers in this regard even if there is some departure from these rules. For example, you will find that some of the broken letters (*muqaṭṭa'āt*), with which some chapters begin, have been considered verses, like: *Alif Lām Mīm*, *Alif Lām Mīm Rā*, *Alif Lām Mīm Ṣād*, Kāf Hāyā Yā 'Ayn Ṣād, Ṭā Sīn Mīm, Yāsīn, Ḥāmīm, and Ṭāhā; at the same time many of them have not been regarded as verses like: *Alif Lām Rā*, *Alif Lām Mīm Rā*, Ṭāsīn, Ṣād, Qāf, *and Nūn*.

The verses of the Qur'ān are different from each other in the number of their words. Some of them are longer than others. Therefore, measuring time with the number of verses, as the Arabs used to say:

---

1 Jalāl al-Dīn 'Abd al-Raḥmān al-Suyūṭī, *al-Itqān*, 1: 271.

2 Abū Dāwūd Sulaymān bin al-Ash'ath, *Sunan Abī Dāwūd* (Riyadh: Dār al-Salām, 1420/1999), 566, ḥadīth no. 4001.

“as much as reciting fifty verses”, could be merely an approximate estimate. And the length of a verse is subject to the requirement of rhetoric which appears from the occasion of the terminal pauses and assumes significance in accordance with the foregoing speech.

The longest verses in the Qur’ān are thus in the following chapters *al-Fath* (Victory) and *al-Baqarah* (Cow):They are the ones who denied Revelation and hindered you from the Sacred Mosque and the sacrificial animals, detained from reaching their place of sacrifice. Had there not been believing men and believing women whom ye did not know that ye were trampling down and on whose account a crime would have accrued to you without (your) knowledge, (Allah would have allowed you to force your way, but He held back your hands) that He may admit to His Mercy whom He will. If they had been apart, We should certainly have punished the Unbelievers among them with a grievous Punishment. While the Unbelievers got up in their hearts heat and cant – the heat and cant of ignorance – Allah sent down His Tranquility to his Messenger and to the Believers, and made them stick close to the command of self-restraint; and well were they entitled to it and worthy of it. And Allah has full knowledge of all things (48:25-26).

They followed what the evil ones gave out (falsely) against the power of Solomon: the blasphemers were, not Solomon, but the evil ones, teaching men Magic, and such things as came down at Babylon to the angels Harut and Marut. But neither of these taught anyone (Such things) without saying: “We are only for trial; so do not blaspheme.” They learned from them the means to sow discord between man and wife. But they could not thus harm anyone except by Allah’s permission. And they learned what harmed them, not what profited them. And they knew that the buyers of (magic) would have no share in the happiness of the Hereafter. And vile was the price for which they did sell their souls, if they but knew! (2:102).

The shortest verse of the Qur’ān with respect to the number of words is *Mudhāmmatān* in the chapter *al-Raḥmān*, and with respect to letters *Ṭāhā* (in the chapter of the same name).

And the pauses (*wuqūf*) in the Qur'ān do not necessarily coincide with the endings of verses. The two have no link with each other. At times, there are a number of pauses in one verse; for example "To Him is referred the Knowledge of the Hour (of Judgment: He knows all): No date-fruit comes out of its sheath, nor does a female conceive (within her womb) (pause) nor bring forth except by His knowledge, the Day that (Allah) will propound to them the (question), "Where are the partners (ye attributed to Me?" They will say, "We do assure thee not one of us can bear witness!" (pause and end of the verse (41:47). At the end of our discussion, we will have more to say about pauses.

As to the difference of opinion among scholars about the total number of verses in the Qur'ān based on their difference about the endings of some verses, it is either due to variation in the reports, as we stated before, or some of it appears due to difference in individual reasoning (*ijtihād*).

In his *Kitāb al-'Adad*, Abū 'Amr al-Dānī says: "there is a consensus that the number of the verses is six thousand. However, there is a difference about verses beyond this number. Some scholars do not increase this number. Some count two hundred and four beyond it. Some count fourteen, some nineteen, some twenty-five, some thirty-six and others took the number up to six hundred and sixteen beyond the agreed six thousand."[1]

In the commentary on *al-Burhān*, al-Māzari says "Makkī bin Abī Ṭālib says: 'the people dealing with numbers have agreed to exclude the counting of *Basmalah* as a verse in the beginning of every chapter. These people include the scholars of Kūfah, Baṣrah, Madīnah and Syria. Their difference is confined to counting it in the first chapter

1 Aḥmad bin Muṣṭafā al-Shahīr bi Ṭāsh Kubrā Zādah, *Muftāh (sic) al-Sa'ādah wa Miṣbāh al-Siyādah fī Mawḍū'āt al-'Ulūm* (Beirut: Dār al-Kutub al-'Ilmiyyah, 1405/1985), 2: 359. It is to be noted, however, that I could not find the abovementioned quotation in the following book of al-Dānī, though he discussed the matter. Abū 'Amr al-Dānī al-Andalusī, *al-Bayān fī 'Add Āyy al-Qur'ān*, ed., Ghānim Qudūrī al-Ḥamd (Kuwait: Manshūrāt Markaz al-Makhṭūṭāt wa al-Turāth wa al-Wathā'iq, 1414/1994), 79-82.

(*al-Ḥamd*) only. The men of Kūfah and Makkah have reckoned it a verse and those of Baṣrah, Syria and Madīnah have not'."[1]

Notwithstanding the minor difference in the counting of verses that often occurs due to including or excluding the *Basmalah* in every chapter, the fact is established that the number of the verses of chapters was known at the time of the Prophet (peace be upon him). Muḥammad bin Sā'ib relates from Ibn 'Abbās (may God be pleased with him) that when the last verse of the Qur'ān was revealed: "And fear the Day when ye shall be brought back to Allah. Then shall every soul be paid what it earned, and none shall be dealt with unjustly" (2:281), Jibrīl (AS) said to the Prophet (peace be upon him) "place it at the head of two hundred and eighty of *Sūrat al-Baqarah*" (i.e. chapter two).[2] There is another tradition cited by al-Bukhārī which proves that the number of verses was quite familiar among the Prophet's Companions. Sa'īd bin Jubayr relates from Ibn 'Abbās (may God be pleased with him) who said "if you wish to be amused by the ignorance of (pre-Islamic) Arabs, then you should read the verse one hundred and thirty in the chapter *al-An'ām* 'Lost are those who slay their children, from folly, without knowledge' (6:140)."[3]

8.2. Order of Verses

As to the ordering of verses one after the other, this had been prescribed by the Prophet (peace be upon him) in accordance with the Divine Revelation. It is a well-known fact that the Qur'ān was revealed

1 Makkī bin Abī Ṭālib al-Qaysī, *Kitāb al-Kashf 'an Wujūh al-Qirā'āt al-Sab' wa 'Ilalihā wa Ḥijajihā*, Muḥy al-Dīn Ramaḍān, ed., 2nd ed. (Beirut: Mu'assasat al-Risālah, 1401/1981), 1: 23; Muḥammad bin 'Alī bin 'Umar bin Muḥammad al-Tamīmī al-Māzarī, *Īḍāḥ al-Maḥṣūl min Burhān al-Uṣūl*, 'Ammār al-Ṭālibī, ed. (n.p.: Dār al-Gharb al-Islāmī, n.d.). Unfortunately, I could not trace the abovementioned quotation in this book. It is also important to note that the editor of the book did not mention the name of Makkī bin Abī Ṭālib, to whom our author had attributed the quotation, in the index of the names. [Ed.]

2 Abū Muḥammad al-Ḥusayn bin Mas'ūd al-Baghawī, *Ma'ālim al-Tanzīl*, Khālid 'Abd al-Raḥmān al-'Akk and Marwān Sawār, eds. (Beirut: Dār al-Ma'rifah, n d), 1: 266; Abū 'Amr al-Dānī al-Andalusī, *al-Bayān fī 'Add Āyy al-Qur'ān*, 38.

3 Muḥammad bin Ismā'īl al-Bukhārī, *Ṣaḥīḥ al-Bukhārī*, 593, ḥadīth no. 3524.

piecemeal in the form of verses. Sometimes, a number of verses were revealed continuously, and at other times a whole chapter was revealed. This order between verses is among the miraculous features of the Qur'ān. And on this order rests the brightness of its unique style.

That is why the order in which verses of chapters have reached us is a definite determined order. Because if this is changed, it will come down from the level of miracle whereby it is distinguished. Therefore, it is a proven fact that the recitation of the Prophet (peace be upon him) was strictly in the same order of verses which is there in the Scripture possessed by the Muslims today. Those Companions who presented recitation of the Qur'ān before the Prophet (peace be upon him) in his last years followed the same order of verses. Last but not least is the fact that when Zayd bin Thābit (may God be pleased with him) wrote the Scripture on the order of Abū Bakr (may God be pleased with him) he did not show any difference in this order of verses.

Those Companions who memorized the Qur'ān in whole or in part followed the order of verses observed in the Prophet's recitation in those prayers in which it is done loudly and on several other occasions. In memorizing the Qur'ān, they relied on their own individual powers of retention. They did not depend on writing in this respect. The scribes of the Revelation, for their part, were engaged in writing whatever was revealed by the command of the Prophet and this was according to the Divine timing. Probably the wisdom in writing was to provide a recourse to the Muslims to verify the text should they ever face any doubt or undergo forgetfulness. When the Qur'ān was compiled at the time of Abū Bakr, it is not reported that the Companions hesitated in the order of verses in any chapter. Nor was any difference expressed by them about whatever was being compiled of the Qur'ān. Because all this was exactly in conformity with what they had memorized of the Book. Ibn Wahb says: "I heard Mālik say: 'the Qur'ān was compiled on the basis of what the Companions used to hear from the Prophet (peace be upon him)'."[1] And Ibn al-Anbārī says: "a verse used to be revealed in reply to a query by someone and Jibrīl used to identify the place of the verse to the Prophet (peace be upon him)."[2] Thus, the order of words, verses and all the chapters have been identified by the Prophet (peace be upon him).

Therefore, the basic feature of the Qur'ānic verses has been that of a certain compatibility between a verse and the following verse or a certain diversion from it to another theme or such other things that are the traits of a well-knit and well-ordered specimen of language. Among the things that indicate this mutual link and complementarity between verses is the presence of various devices of conjunction such as *fā'*, *lākin*, and *bal*, and the devices of exemption, all of which show this link. Though the presence of these devices by no means indicates the mutual relation of verses in respect of revelation. For it so happened that the words "and receive no hurt" are three words in the Qur'ān that were revealed after the previous and subsequent parts of the verse were revealed. And these three words are very much connected to the rest of the verse.

Al-Zarkashi says "some of our teachers have said: 'it is a wrong notion held by some people that compatibility should not be searched between the verses.' On the contrary, what should be done with each verse is that one should first of all search its compatibility with the previous and the subsequent verse. In case one finds a verse self-sufficient and self-contained, he should still search its relevance to the previous discourse. In this quest for compatibility lies the key for abundant hidden knowledge."[3]

It could also be rarely the case that there might not be any compatibility between verses in respect of their meaning and message. But some particular reason has been the cause of placing a verse where

---

1 Jalāl al-Dīn 'Abd al-Raḥmān al-Suyūṭī, *al-Itqān*, 1: 194.

2 Ibid., 1: 195.

3 Muḥammad bin 'Abd Allāh al-Zarkashī, *al-Burhān fī 'Ulūm al-Qur'ān*, 1: 37.

it is placed. For example, the words "(The angels say:) 'We descend not but by command of thy Lord'" (19:64) are explained by a report according to which the Prophet (peace be upon him) had expressed to Jibrīl (AS) his sadness over the long interval in the Revelation. In response to that, these words were revealed after the words "Such is the Garden which We give as an inheritance to those of Our servants who guard against Evil" (19:63).

Similarly, the objection by the polytheists over the employment of the simile of a mosquito was answered in the verse: "Allah disdains not to use the similitude of things, lowest as well as highest" (2:26), which came after the verse:

But give glad tidings to those who believe and work righteousness, that their portion is Gardens, beneath which rivers flow. Every time they are fed with fruits therefrom, they say: "Why, this is what we were fed with before," for they are given things in similitude; and they have therein Companions pure (and holy); and they abide therein (forever) (2:25).

Thus, either there should be a compatibility between the verse and its *infra* and *supra* or there should be found a particular reason for placing a verse in its position. Another example of the above case is the verse "Move not thy tongue concerning the (Qur'an) to make haste therewith" (75:16) which has come in the chapter *al-Qiyāma*, the theme of which is a rebuke of the polytheists over their denial of the resurrection. This is followed by a description of the dreadful scenes of Doomsday. There is no compatibility of the above verse (75:16) with this theme. But the cause of its revelation had occurred during the revelation itself. As al-Bukhārī reports from Ibn 'Abbās (may God be pleased with him) who relates "when Jibrīl (AS) came with the Revelation, the Prophet (peace be upon him) used to move his tongue and lips in his effort to memorize the revealed verses. Thereupon, Allah revealed this verse (75:16) in this chapter (75)."[1]

1 Muḥammad bin Ismā'īl al-Bukhārī, *Ṣaḥīḥ al-Bukhārī*, 878, ḥadīth no. 4929.

This report shows that the Prophet (peace be upon him) had moved his tongue and lips in the recitation of the verses in the beginning of this chapter.

Therefore, the non-appearance of a compatibility between a verse and the foregoing one should not bewilder any *mufassir*. Because this might be due to some reason that has coincided with the revelation of the verse along which it has been placed in the appropriate position by the Prophet (peace be upon him). And obviously this placement by the Prophet (peace be upon him) is in accordance with the symmetrical order of the Qur'ān.

However, since the reports regarding the placement of verses by the Prophet (peace be upon him) in particular places are not too many, therefore, it remains the duty of every scholar of *tafsīr* to search for the mutual coherence of the verses as far as it is convenient for him. Nevertheless, he need not labor with artificial reasons to show this coherence.

The foremost purpose of the Qur'ān is to reform the Ummah in totality. The reform of the non-believers has been done by inviting them to belief, to reject the misguided worship and to pursue the path of faith and obedience. And the reform of the believers was done by correcting their morals, setting them on the path of guidance and showing them the ways of success and purification of their souls.

Since the objective of the Revelation was connected with the conditions of the society during the period of the Prophet's mission, the verses of the Qur'ān were independent from each other. Because each verse aimed at the purpose of reform and establishing argument in favor of reform. At the same time, it aimed at foreclosing the doors of misguidance contrary to the intended reform. Therefore, it was not necessary that the verses of the Qur'ān be sent down in a continuum. On the contrary, the status of the Qur'ān is similar to an orator dealing with mutable conditions obtaining at the time of the Revelation and shifting from one condition to another by a mutual link between them.

This is why there are many intervening sentences in the Qur'ān required by the situation or even without it. Every sentence in the Qur'ān thus contains some word of wisdom, guidance or correction of some mistake. For example, the Qur'ān says:

A section of the People of the Book say: "Believe in the morning what is revealed to the believers, but reject it at the end of the day; perchance they may (themselves) turn back; and believe no one unless he follows your religion." Say: "True guidance is the Guidance of Allah" (3:72-73).

In this verse, the words "True guidance is the Guidance of Allah" have come as an intervening sentence.

8.3. Pauses in the Qur'ān

A pause (*waqf*) is to break the voice on a word for such duration as is sufficient normally for taking breath. A pause at the end of a Qur'ānic sentence might be the basis of meaning originally conveyed by the speech. Therefore, a change in pause will alter the meaning. For example, the Qur'ān says "but no one knows its hidden meanings except Allah. And those who are firmly grounded in knowledge say: 'We believe in the Book'" (3:7). If someone pauses at إِلَّا ٱللَّهُ (except Allah), then it would mean that the figurative statements are known to Allah exclusively like the knowledge of the Hour etc. And the subsequent part of the verse will be the beginning of a new statement meaning that the well-versed scholars attribute this knowledge to Allah. And if the words إِلَّا ٱللَّهُ (except Allah) are joined with the subsequent part of the verse, then it would mean that the well-versed scholars indeed know the meaning of the figurative statements of the Qur'ān and at the same time they say "we believe therein."

And at all the presumptions, you will not find in the Qur'ān any place where pause is obligatory and not prohibited, as Ibn al-Jazarī has pointed out in his *Urjūzah*.[1] But the pauses are classified into strongly recommended and less than that. All this classification is determined by the relevant meaning. Some people prefer to pause at the end of a statement and to make a slight pause without full pause where the meaning of the verse so requires. The latter is a pause less than the one made at the end of a statement. This is because Arabic is a succinct language and the context of the statement sufficiently guards against any incorrect comprehension by an inaccurate pause. For example, if someone pauses at الرسول (the Prophet) in the verse "… and have (on the contrary) driven out the Prophet and yourselves (from your homes), (simply) because ye believe in Allah your Lord!" (60:1), then this pause would not mean a warning against believing in Allah, especially because the word Allah in this verse is followed by the adjective: your Lord.'[2] However, there is little doubt that a change in pause may affect the meaning sometimes. This change is like the one that occurs with a different recitation even though the words remain the same.

The matter of pauses in the Qur'ān is also a significant aspect of the linguistic miracle of the Qur'ān. Because the miraculous features include stylistic embellishments among other things. And an important feature of the Qur'ānic style is exhibited in the rhymed endings of verses in some chapters. As we noted above in the discussion on the verses, these rhymed endings are integral to the rhetorical symmetry of the Qur'ān. Therefore, failure to observe the required pauses in the Qur'ān is indeed an omission in observing an important purpose of the Qur'ān.

The early scholars did not concern themselves much with determining the pauses because the matter was obvious and

---

1 Muḥammad bin Muḥammad bin 'Alī bin Yūsuf Ibn al-Jazarī, *Manẓūmat al-Jazariyyah* (n.p.: Shu'bat Taw'iyat al-Jāliyāt bi al-Zulfā, n.d.), 19-20, verse no. 78; Muḥammad Ismā'īl al-Khundawī, *al-Aqwāl al-Imdādiyyah 'alā Muqaddimat al-Jazariyyah bi al-Su'āl wa al-Jawāb* (Lahore: al-Maktabah al-Imdādiyyah al-Tajwīdiyyah, 1394/1974), 169.

2 A literal rendering of the verse, should one pause at الرسول (the Prophet) 'al-Rasūl', would be 'Beware of believing in Allah your Lord'. (Ed.)

self-evident. However, reflecting on the endings of verses was of more interest to them due to their rhetorical significance as an established evidence of the miracle of the Qur'ān. It was when many commoners of the Arabs and other people entered Islam that the scholars of the Qur'ān addressed the issue of determining the pauses to facilitate their comprehension by the reciters of the Qur'ān. The most famous of the scholars who contributed to this aspect of the Qur'ān's study were: Abū Muḥammad bin Al-Anbārī and Abū Ja'far bin al-Nuḥās.[1] The author of the famous work *al-Itqān* also refers to a work on this subject by one al-Nikzāwī or al-Nikzawī.[2] Among the later scholars from North Africa Muḥammad bin Abī Jumu'at al-Habaṭī is very well-known.

8.4. Chapters of the Qur'ān

A *sūrah* (i.e. chapter) is a unit in the Qur'ān with a definite beginning and end which are immutable. Each chapter has been given a particular name and contains at least three verses, with a complete theme focused by the meanings of its verses. Either a chapter originates from an occasion of the revelation or required by something in the contents of that chapter.

And its consisting of at least three verses is derived from a survey of the chapters of the Qur'*ān along* with a report of 'Umar (may God be pleased with him) transmitted by [Ibn] Abī Dāwūd. According to this report, when 'Umar (may God be pleased with him) was visited by Ḥārith bin Khuzaymah (mentioned in some reports as Abū Khuzaymah or Khuzaymah) and informed him of the last two verses of the chapter *Barā'ah*, he (i.e. 'Umar) remarked "if these were three verses, I would have made them a separate chapter."[3] This shows that he knew that this was the minimum quantum of a chapter. The name *sūrah* for the

1 Jalāl al-Dīn 'Abd al-Raḥmān al-Suyūṭī, *al-Itqān*, 1: 258-59.

2 Ibid.

3 'Abd Allāh bin Abī Dāwūd Sulaymān bin al-Ash'ath al-Sijistānī, *Kitāb al-Maṣāḥif*, ed. Arthur Jeffery (n.p.: al-Maṭba'at al-Raḥmāniyyah, 1355/1936), 30; Aḥmad bin 'Alī bin Ḥajar al-'Asqalānī, *Fatḥ al-Bārī Sharḥ Ṣaḥīḥ al-Bukhārī*, 9: 20.

chapters of the Qur'ān is a term coined by the Qur'ān itself. And this name became famous among the Arabs, even the Polytheists. When the Qur'ān challenged them to "produce one *sūrah* like in the Qur'ān," they knew what it meant. Also the verses containing this challenge were revealed subsequent to the first chapters of the Qur'ān. And the name of the chapter "*Nūr*" is mentioned as *sūrah* in the opening of that chapter itself. The *sunnah* has further explicated its meaning. As to the parts of *Tawrāh*, *Injīl* and *Zabūr*, these were never named *sūrah* in pre-Islamic or post-Islamic times.

The reason for naming a certain unit of the Qur'ān *sūrah* is said to have originated from the word *sūr* which means the wall that encloses a city or a part of it. *Hā* has been added at the end to convey the sense of a piece. It is like giving the name of *khuṭbah* (sermon), *risālah* (letter), or *muqāmah* (literary narrative) to a particular piece of language. The plural of *sūrah* is *suwar*.

Organizing the Qur'ān into *sūrah*s has been based on the *sunnah* since the Prophet's era, as the Qur'ān had been divided into one hundred fourteen chapters with their names from that time. The majority of the Prophet's Companions had agreed on this division of the Qur'ān into one hundred fourteen chapters at the time of its compilation by them. According to a tradition reported by the authors of *Sunan* on the authority of Ibn 'Abbās, when a verse was revealed, the Prophet (peace be upon him) used to say "put this in such chapter."[1] And he used to identify the chapter. Therefore, these chapters were identified with their volumes since the Prophet's time and these were preserved in the prescribed recitation in the Prayers and during the public recital of the Qur'ān by the Prophet (peace be upon him) and by others under his supervision. Thus the order of the verses into chapters was done at the instruction of the Prophet. In the same way, the total number of the chapters is also established by the word of the Prophet (peace be upon him). This fact is further supported by many reports in the *Ṣaḥīḥ*

---

1 Aḥmad bin 'Alī bin Ḥajar al-'Asqalānī, *Fatḥ al-Bārī Sharḥ Ṣaḥīḥ al-Bukhārī*, 9: 12.

wherein it has been said that the Prophet (peace be upon him) recited in the Prayers such and such chapters from the long and short sections of the chapters.[1] The benefits of dividing the Qur'*ān into chapters include, as pointed out by the author of al-Kashshāf*, while explaining the verse "then produce a *sūrah* like thereunto" (2:23), "if an element is divided into subdivisions, it is better and nobler than one continuous statement. When a reader completes one chapter or section of a book and starts reading another, it refreshes him and energizes his feelings like a traveler when he discovers that he has covered the distance of a mile or more."[2]

Also, in places, there are verses in the Qur'ān that indicate the precedence of one foregoing chapter to another. For example, the verse of the chapter *al-Naḥl* ("The Bee") which reads: "To the Jews We prohibited such things as We have mentioned to thee before" (16:118) points to another verse in the chapter *al-An'ām* "For those who followed the Jewish Law, We forbade every (animal) with undivided hoof" (6:146). This cross-referencing shows that the chapter *al-An'ām* was revealed before the chapter *al-Naḥl.* And it is placed in the same order in the Qur'ān. Similarly, it is established that the last verse of the Qur'ān belongs either to the chapter *al-Baqarah* (The Cow), *al-Nisā'* (The Women) or *al-Barā'ah* (immunity) and all the three chapters are prior to so many chapters.

The early scripts written by the Companions for themselves during the Prophet's lifetime had been different in the order of the chapters. These include the scripts of 'Abd Allāh bin Mas'ūd and Ubayy bin Ka'b. Another Companion Sālim Mawlā Abī Ḥudhayfah is reported to be the first to have collected the whole Qur'ān in a script.[3] The author of *al-Itqān* says "there were some Companions who had prepared their scripts according to the order of revelation-that is-in accordance with

1 Muḥammad bin 'Īsā al-Tirmidhī, *Jāmi' al-Tirmidhī*, 83-84, ḥadīths no. 306-10.
2 Maḥmūd bin 'Umar al-Zamakhsharī, *al-Kashshāf*, 1: 219.
3 Jalāl al-Dīn 'Abd al-Raḥmān al-Suyūṭī, *al-Itqān*, 1: 183-84.

the knowledge reaching them. Similar was the order followed by ‘Alī (may God be pleased with him) in his script. Thus it started with *Iqra’* followed by *al-Muddaththir*, *al-Muzzammil*, *al-Takwīr* and so on up to the last chapter revealed at Makka and then followed by the Madinan chapters. There were some who had arranged their scripts according to the long and short chapters. The same was the order of chapters maintained in the scripts of Ubayy and Ibn Mas‘ūd. They started with *al-Baqarah* followed by *al-Nisā’* then *Āl-‘Imran*."[1] And in the same order, ‘Uthm*ān (may God be pleased with him) had instructed that the master-script (al-Muṣḥaf al-Imām*) should be written. However, the consensus of the majority has been established on the fact that most of the chapters of the Qur’ān had been already arranged in the correct order during the Prophet’s own life-time. Also a number of traditions in the *Ṣaḥīḥ* of Bukhārī and Muslim that report recitation of various chapters in the prayer by the Prophet (peace be upon him) support this general consensus.[2] In this respect, we find a clear and emphatic statement of Shams al-D*īn Maḥmūd al-Asfahānī al-Shāfi‘ī*. He says in the fifth introduction to his work on *Tafsīr* "there is no disagreement over the fact that the Qur’ān is essentially transmitted through an uninterrupted overwhelming chain of narrators (*mutawātir*) both in its essence as well as in its parts. Its internal order and arrangement also enjoys the same high status of authenticity according to the learned scholars." This is simply because the requirements and circumstances fully favored its uninterrupted transmission. While the order of verses and chapters in the Qur’ān has been established on the basis of this strong evidence, still many scholars have been of the view that in reciting it, it is not obligatory to observe this order. At best it has been considered recommended to do so. It may be noted that the division of the chapters into long and short ones has been made mainly on the basis of the number of verses, not of words or letters. There is, however,

1 Ibid., 1: 195.
2 Muḥammad bin Ismā‘īl al-Bukhārī, *Ṣaḥīḥ al-Bukhārī*, 123-26, ḥadīths no. 758-76; Muslim bin al-Ḥajjāj bin Muslim al-Qushayrī, *Ṣaḥīḥ Muslim*, 191-94, ḥadīths no. 1022-43.

some difference of opinion with regard to the Makkan and Madinan chapters of the Qur'ān, though this difference is negligible. In the arrangement of the Scripture, the Makkan and Madinan chapters overlap. As to the order of revelation of these chapters, there are three reports about it, all traceable to Ibn 'Abbās. These reports have been transmitted by Mujāhid, 'Aṭā' al-Khurāsānī and Jābir bin Zayd. The latter has been relied upon by al-Ja'barī in his versified treatise entitled *Taqrīb al-Ma'mūl fī Tartīb al-Nuzūl.*[1] Al-Suyūṭī has also acknowledged it in his work *al-Itqān*[2] and we have followed it in this *tafsīr*.

As to the names of the chapters, these had been assigned to them since the time of the Revelation. The purpose of naming the chapters was to facilitate reference and remembrance. The report of Ibn 'Abbās cited above to the effect that when a verse was revealed, the Prophet (peace be upon him) used to say "place it in the chapter in which such and such things are mentioned," also supports this fact. The benefit of assigning names to chapters is that a chapter is thereby distinguishable from other chapters.

Apparently, the Companions assigned names to the chapters on the basis of what they learnt from the Prophet (peace be upon him) or adopted the most famous names whereby people knew some chapters even though these names might not have been transmitted. However, the names of many chapters had become famous at the time of the Prophet (peace be upon him) and he had heard and confirmed them.

Sometimes, the names of chapters are taken from the features of the chapters like *al-Fātiḥah* and *Sūrat al-Ḥamd*. At other times, a chapter is named by its attribution to something that is mentioned in it like the chapters *Luqmān*, *Yūsuf* and *al-Baqarah*. Sometimes, a chapter is named after something that is mentioned in it in greater detail like the chapters *Hūd* and *Ibrāhīm*. Also some chapters take their names from some words that occur in them like *Barā'ah*, *Ḥā Mīm*, *Ḥā Mīm 'Ayn*

---

1 Jalāl al-Dīn 'Abd al-Raḥmān al-Suyūṭī, *al-Itqān*, 1: 82-84.

2 Ibid., 1: 81-82.

Sīn Qāf, *Ḥā Mīm al-Sajdah*, as some early scholars had called it, and *al-Fāṭir*.

It should be noted that the Companions did not write in the Scripture the names of chapters. They only wrote *Basmalah* in the beginning of each chapter to distinguish between two chapters. They did so because they did not like to write in between the Qur'ān something that was not a verse of the Qur'ān. Therefore, they adopted *Basmalah* as it was appropriate for inaugurating a chapter and it was also a verse of the Qur'ān. Then in the period of the successors of the Companions (*tābi'ūn*) the names of the chapters were written in the scriptures and no one objected to it.

As to the order of the verses in the chapter, it is a known fact that the revelation was piecemeal as already noted above. This process of gradual revelation was maintained both in the verses and the chapters. At times, some chapters were revealed all at once like the chapter *al-Fātiḥah* and *al-Mursalāt* among the short chapters. At other times, some chapters were intermittently revealed like *al-An'ām*. Sometimes, a chapter was revealed in parts and at others two of them were revealed in parts on different overlapping occasions.[1] Al-Tirmidhī reports from 'Uthmān bin 'Affān on the authority of Ibn 'Abbās, who said "there used to come upon the Prophet (peace be upon him) times when many chapters were revealed to him intermittently. When something was revealed to him, he would call those who used to transcribe the Revelation and would say to them: 'Place these verses in such and such chapters'."[2] This is why some chapters are partly Makkan and partly Madinan. In the same way, the end of the chapters was also determined by the instructions of the Prophet (peace be upon him). Thus the ends of the chapters were quite known. When the Prophet (peace be upon him) died, the Qur'ān had been already well organized into definite chapters.

---

1 Ibid., 1: 119-20.

2 Muḥammad bin 'Īsā al-Tirmidhī, *Jāmi' al-Tirmidhī*, 695, ḥadīth no. 3086.

The Companions who had compiled the whole of the Qur'ān in the life-time of the Prophet (peace be upon him) were: Zayd bin Thābit, Mu'adh bin Jabal, Abū Zayd, Ubayy bin Ka'b, Abū al-Dardā', 'Abd Allāh bin 'Umar, 'Ubādah bin al-Ṣāmit, Abū Ayyūb, Sa'd bin 'Ubayd, Mujammi' bin Jāriyah, and Abū Mūsā al-Ash'arī.[1] And a large number of the Companions had memorized most of the Qur'ān with difference in quantity.

1 Jalāl al-Dīn 'Abd al-Raḥmān al-Suyūṭī, *al-Itqān*, 1: 226-27.

CHAPTER NINE

SEMANTIC SCOPE OF THE QUR'ĀN

The Arabs have had a natural instinct for discernment and understanding. On the basis of this inherent intelligence evolved their modes of language, especially the language employed by those among them who were masters of rhetorical speech. That is why conciseness and brevity were the main pillars of their rhetoric since the users of language trusted the intelligence of their audience. This quality of the Arabs is reflected in the proverbial words "a signifying flash". That is why the use of metaphor, figurative speech, illustrative expression, metonymy, insinuation, exaggeration, diversion, significant allusion, declarative clause for other purposes and interrogative clause for affirmation or denial and similar things had been abundant in their language.

The essence of all this is creation of abundant meaning and expressing of the mental meaning by the speaker in the most clear and concise phrase that clings to the mind. The Qur'ān was the Revelation by the All-Knowing. He intended it to be a sign of the truthfulness of His Prophet (peace be upon him). He challenged the masters of eloquence among the Arabs to emulate its shortest chapter; it has been, therefore, composed in a matchless symmetry to the utmost capacity of Arabic language to present subtleties and profundities of language both in word and meaning. In this way, it fulfilled the highest purpose of communication in communicating its message to its addressees.

Thus the Qur'ān came with the most innovative style the Arabs were familiar with and bewildered them. It rendered its opponents, who were masters of rhetoric, unable to emulate its style. They had no option but to surrender before its majesty of speech and eloquence of expression. Some of their most prominent men of letters embraced

Islam under its miraculous impact, like Labīd bin Rabī'ah, Ka'b bin Zuhayr and al-Nābighah al-Ja'dī, while others stubbornly continued to oppose it, like Walīd bin Mughīrah. Thus, the miracle of the Qur'ān enfolded most of the familiar meanings that the Arab masters of rhetoric employed in their language. And since the Qur'ān is a Book of legislation, teaching and instruction, it was appropriate that it should be invested with meaning and message to the utmost capacity of words within the minimum number of them. This was done with the linguistic resources of the Arabic language, which happens to be the richest of all lexicons in this respect. In this way, the purpose of guiding people in all spheres of guidance was fully attained.

The pattern adopted by the masters of eloquence was to invest their speech with all the meaning that the aim of that speech required and to leave the rest. In the case of the Qur'ān, it was appropriate that it should compress in its fold the whole message that its listeners were in need of knowing. And in addition to that, it encompassed all those elements that contributed to rhetorical excellence of variant patterns. In these patterns of rhetorical communication, sometimes the main purport of speech is intended *per se* while secondary meanings are also conveyed alongside the former. Also at times, the construction of words conveys both meanings – primary and secondary – with equal clarity and succinctness; and at others, these differ in that respect to the extent of falling in the category of hermeneutic interpretation (*ta'wīl*). The latter consists in assigning a meaning to the word on the basis of a less probable connotation.

In case the two meanings are equal in terms of connotation, then the matter becomes clearer. For example, the Qur'ān says "for of a surety they killed him not" (4:157), which could mean: "they did not kill him but thought so"; or it could mean: "those Christians who differed about the murder of 'Īsā did not have any certain knowledge of facts, hence they understood the matter wrongly". Another example of this is the verse: "But Satan made him forget to mention him to his lord" (12:42). The words *dhikr* and *rabbihī* convey two meanings both of which are valid. The first meaning is "then Satan made him forget to remember his master." And the second is "then Satan made him forget the remembrance of his Lord" (i.e. Allah. In the same way, the word *Rabb* occurring in the verse: "He said: 'Allah forbid! truly he is my lord! he made my sojourn agreeable!'" (12:23) could have two meanings that are both valid and applicable. At times, the meanings increase by applying the word of a verse to two or more connotations for the sake of yielding multiple meanings with brevity of the text. And this feature of the Qur'ān is among its miraculous qualities. For example, the words of the Qur'ān: "... only because of a promise he had made to him" (9:114); in these words there is more than one possibility about the subject of the promise.

The Qur'ān has come down from the All-Knowing whose knowledge encompasses all things. Therefore, all the constructions that accord with the Arabs' conventions of eloquence and rhetorical communication and carry meanings familiar to the Arabs in those constructions, will be considered included and intended in these constructions. However, a connotation that is disapproved by any explicit or predominant factor sanctioned by the *sharī'ah*, rules of the language or express command of religious authority, shall be precluded from this principle. Allah has made the Qur'ān the Book that contains guidance for the whole *Ummah*. He has invited them to reflect on it and to exhaust their effort in deriving meanings from it. This invitation has been reiterated in so many verses of the Qur'ān. Moreover, the Qur'ān is the ultimate source of evidence for the commands of the *sharī'ah* that is recognized as such by all the scholars of Islam.

Some explanations of the Qur'ānic verses that have been provided by the Prophet (peace be upon him), as reported in the traditions, lend support to the above contention. When we look at these explanations, we find that these are not the immediate connotations of these verses. When we ponder them further, we notice that what the Prophet (peace be upon him) intended was to awaken the minds to discover the deeper layers of meaning from the words of the Qur'ān. An example of this is the tradition reported by Abū Sa'īd bin al-Mu'allā. He says "Once the Prophet (peace be upon him) called me while I was busy in praying. Therefore, I could not respond to his call. After concluding the prayer, I went to him. He said to me: 'what prevented you from responding to me?' I said: 'O Prophet of Allah: I was praying'. The Prophet (peace be upon him) said 'did not Allah say: "give your response to Allah and His Messenger, when He calleth you" (8:24)?'"[1] Now there is little doubt that the meaning intended in this verse is responding in the sense of obeying as indicated in other verses also. And the meaning of "calling" is "guiding" as shown by other verses too. But since the word *istijābah* (responding) was fit to be used in its literal sense i.e. "responding to a summons", the Prophet (peace be upon him) applied the above verse to a situation fit for it, without reference to the object mentioned in it in the words: "to that which will give you life" (8:24).

Also included in this category, for example, is the saying of the Prophet (peace be upon him) "people will be resurrected on the Doomsday bare-footed, naked and exposed", "as We began the first creation, We will return them to that state" (21:104).[2]

Now in the words of the Qur'ān employed by the Prophet (peace be upon him), there is simile in which the second creation (resurrection) has been likened to the first creation in order to dispel improbability of resurrection. However, since this simile was useful to liken the latter state (resurrection) to the former (creation *ex nihilo*) in all respects, the Prophet (peace be upon him) informed us in this saying, that this sense is also implied in the above verse. Thus the likening of the resurrected souls to their first creation should include their being stripped of dress and shoes.

Another example of this is found in the Prophet's saying to Umm Kulthūm bint 'Uqba bin Mu'īṭ when she migrated to Madīnah after embracing Islam and refusing to return to the polytheists: "It is He

---

1 Muḥammad bin Ismā'īl al-Bukhārī, *Ṣaḥīḥ al-Bukhārī*, 759, ḥadīth no. 4474.

2 Ibid., 559, ḥadīth no. 3349.

Who brings out the living from the dead" (30:19). In this verse, the Prophet (peace be upon him) employed its metaphorical meaning, which is other than its literal meaning intended in the verse. I also find the Prophet's act of prostrating on certain occasions in the Qur'ān (*sujūd al-tilāwah*) to be founded on this very principle. If this act was performed by the Prophet's own understanding, then it is pursuant to this principle as explained above. But if this act of prostration was prescribed by Divine inspiration, then this is a stronger evidence that Allah did intend by the words of His Book such other meanings as its words are capable of, provided, of course, that these meanings do not violate the objectives of the Revelation.

Another instance of the extended application of a verse is that during one of the battles, 'Amr bin al-'Āṣ became obliged to take bath on a cool day. He performed *tayammum* saying that Allah states: "Nor kill (or destroy) yourselves: for verily Allah hath been to you Most Merciful" (4:29).[1] Now this verse actually prohibits mutual killing among people. But 'Amr bin al-'Āṣ extended its application to all situations of apprehending death. In the same way, 'Umar bin al-Khaṭṭāb had derived the beginning of Islamic calendar on the basis of the day of the Prophet's migration to Madīnah from the verse "There is a mosque whose foundation was laid from the first day on piety; it is more worthy of standing forth (for prayer) therein" (9:108).[2] Now, the real meaning of the verse is that "this mosque was established from the *first day* on the basis of *taqwa*". However, the words could also mean that the mosque was built on the day that was most fit to be the first day of the Islamic era. Thus this "firstness" of the day was used by 'Umar bin al-Khaṭṭāb in a relative sense not in a chronological sense. Also we find that our jurists have argued for the validation of the contracts of *ja'ālah* and *kafālah* (consideration and surety) from the verse "for him who produces it, is (the reward of) a camel load; I will be bound by it"

1 Ibid., 60.
2 Ismā'īl bin Kathīr, *al-Sīrah al-Nabawiyyah*, Muṣṭafā 'Abd al-Wāḥid, ed. (Beirut: Dār al-Ma'rifah li al-Ṭibā'ah wa al-Nashr, 1396/1976), 2: 287-89.

(12:72).[1] This despite the fact that it is a narration of a past story of a bygone people stating something neither in affirmation nor in negation. However, since the Qur'ān mentioned it as it was without following it with any disapprobation, it served as a source for deriving the above legal rules.

In the same category falls the argument derived by Imām Shāfi'ī in favor of consensus as a binding source of law from the following verse: "If anyone contends with the Messenger even after guidance has been plainly conveyed to him, and follows a path other than that becoming to men of Faith, We shall leave him in the path he has chosen, and land him in Hell,- what an evil refuge" (4:115),[2] even though the context of the verse pertains to the state of the polytheists. Despite the particular connotation of the verse, Imām Shāfi*'ī* derived from its totality of meaning, evidence in support of consensus as a binding source of law.

Also those modes of recital that have been established by a continuous chain of transmitters, if they differ in reciting words of the Qur'ān in a way that leads to a difference in their connotations, then this variety of meaning is also justified by the same principle.

Further, the meanings of those constructions that carry more than one connotation, their mutual relationship is to be considered that of the general (*al-'umūm*) and the specific (*al-khuṣūṣ*). Provided there is nothing in the text or the context which prevents some connotation. An example of this is to apply the verse "And if any strive (with might and main), they do so for their own souls" (29:6) to "struggling against the lower self for the sake of establishing the ordinances of Islam as well as to fighting the enemies for the defense of Islamic sanctuaries at the same time." Sometimes, there is a conflict between these varied applications in the sense that, if a construction is

1 Zayn al-Dīn al-Shahīr bi Ibn al-Nujaym, *al-Baḥr al-Rā'iq Sharḥ Kanz al-Daqā'iq* (Quetta: al-Maktabat al-Mājidiyyah, n.d.), 6: 208.

2 'Abd al-Malik bin 'Abd Allāh bin Yūsuf al-Juwaynī, *al-Burhān fī Uṣūl al-Fiqh*, 1: 677.

specifically applied to something, it runs contrary to applying it to something else according to the conventions with regard to the intentions of the speaker. But in view of the capacity of a particular construction to yield a variety of meanings, the whole expanse of meanings is adopted by the listener in the hope of absorbing all possibilities of connotation that might have been implied by the speaker. This general application is similar to what the scholars of jurisprudence have said in that "a word or phrase capable of varied meanings should be applicable to all those meanings for the sake of greater caution." At times, the second meaning is created by the first meaning. The latter is doubtlessly included in the framework of meanings because it is connected with the very construction of words, like metonym and insinuation. An example of this is the interpretation put forward by 'Abd Allāh bin 'Abbās (may God be pleased with him) that the chapter *al-Naṣr* points to the imminent demise of the Prophet (peace be upon him). This interpretation was endorsed by 'Umar (may God be pleased with him) as well.[1]

Quite often one comes across a verse and, upon reflection, abundant meanings of the verse come to mind that are all permitted by the construction of words. All these meanings are indicated by views taken from different perspectives that are all valid in the Arabic usage. In such a case when the meanings are numerous and all are permitted by the construction, then one of them need not be considered in conflict with the other. Each meaning is valid in its place. Therefore, all the meanings admissible in the Qur'ānic words, constructions, syntactical order and semantics, including words with multiple meanings, literal and metaphorical, explicit and implicit, figures of speech, conjugation and pause – if these do not run counter to the aim of the context – then the phrase should be understood to include all those meanings. For example, two meanings indicated by two different pauses in the words of *Sūrat al-Baqarah*: "in it is guidance sure, without doubt, for those

---

1 Muḥammad bin Jarīr al-Ṭabarī, *Jāmi' al-Bayān 'an Ta'wīl Āyy al-Qur'ān*, 10: 8816-17.

who fear Allah" (2:2) are valid, whether one pauses at *lā rayb* or at *lā rayba fīh*. The first pause would offer the following meaning: "this is the Book no doubt ...." The second would mean "this is the Book in which there is no doubt. It is a guidance for the righteous." A similar example is the difference in meaning created by different pauses in the following words of the Qur'ān: "none knows its explanation except Allah and those well-versed in knowledge" (3:7). This meaning is indicated if one pauses at "knowledge", however, a different, but equally valid meaning is yielded if one pauses at the Name of Allah. In the latter case, it would mean that Allah alone knows the explanation of figurative verses of the Qur'ān' (*mutashābihāt*).

In short, Allah, the Most High has meant the Qur'ān to be a Book addressing all peoples through the ages. He, therefore, sent it in the most eloquent of all languages, namely Arabic. For this is a language that is richest in its linguistic capital and vocabulary, with least number of letters, yet highest in eloquent expression. Also this language has the greatest capacity for variation in style for the purposes of persuasive communication. Thus Allah made His Book so comprehensive as to include an abundance of meaning that is supplied by its system of composition within the minimum amount of that composition. The stylistic forte of the Qur'ān is, therefore, based on brevity.

Among the most profound features of Qur'ānic diction worthy of note here is its employment of a word that shares two or more meanings all of which are intended simultaneously. It includes using a word in both literal and metaphorical, explicit and implicit meanings. The latter has been identified and stressed by those scholars who have dealt with the Stylistics and Rhetoric. Discussions among the scholars of the Qur'ān have involved different views about the use of words with more than one meaning and the use of literal and metaphorical meanings. The reason for this difference in views is that this use was not known among the Arabs before the revelation of the Qur'ān except quite rarely. Some scholars consider such an extended application of Qur'ānic words a great error.

That is why we find different views among the scholars of Arabic and the jurists of Islam on the validity of explaining one word in a variety of meanings at the same time.

In this regard, we find the following statement of Ghazālī and Abū al-Ḥusayn al-Baṣrī who say "a word that shares multiple meanings may be considered to carry those meanings simultaneously provided it is the intention of the speaker and not merely something indicated by the semantics."[1] My understanding is that they are aiming to link the speaker's intention with the auxiliary meanings conveyed by the very construction of words. Because this link is based on reason and does not need any other circumstance or factor to show it, as in the case of the meanings conveyed by metaphors and figurative speech.

In truth, a polysemous word signifies all or some of its meanings in the linguistic sense. Some people have opined that this application to multiple meanings should be considered as having a literal sense. This opinion is attributed to Imām Shāfi'ī, Abū Bakr al-Bāqillānī and the majority of the *Mu'tazilah* scholars.[2] While some other people have regarded such a multiple application as metaphor.[3] These people said so on the grounds that a word that carries multiple meanings could not be applied to more than one meaning except on the basis of a supportive circumstance (*qarīnah*). This led men like Ibn al-Ḥājib to suppose that since a supportive circumstance was a sign of metaphor, therefore, the word under discussion should also be treated as a metaphor.[4] However, Ibn al-Ḥājib and those who shared his view were mistaken in this view. Because in a metaphor, a circumstance that is regarded as its sign serves as a cause for precluding a literal connotation. Since in the

---

1 'Alī bin 'Abd al-Kāfī al-Subkī and 'Abd al-Wahhāb bin 'Alī al-Subkī, *al-Ibhāj fī Sharḥ al-Minhāj*, Aḥmad Jamāl al-Zamzamī and Nūr al-Dīn 'Abd al-Jabbār Ṣaghīrī, eds. (Dubai: Dār al-Buḥūth li al-Dirāsāt al-Islāmiyyah wa Iḥyā' al-Turāth, 1424/2004), 3: 656.

2 'Abd al-'Azīz al-Bukhārī, *Kashf al-Asrār* (n.p.: al-Maktab al-Ṣanāyi', 1307 AH), 1: 40.

3 Ibid.

4 'Alī bin 'Abd al-Kāfī al-Subkī and 'Abd al-Wahhāb bin 'Alī al-Subkī, *al-Ibhāj fī Sharḥ al-Minhāj*, 3: 656-57.

present case, a word is applied to multiple meanings at once without precluding any of them, therefore, the peculiar condition of metaphor does not apply here.

There is another opinion attributed to Burhān al-Dīn 'Alī al-Marghīnānī, the Ḥanafī jurist and the author of the famous work *al-Hidāyah*. He says that a word carrying multiple meanings could be applied to all those meanings only when the statement is negative.[1]

In short, the most reliable position in the matter is that both a word singly and a composition of words that occur in the Qur'ān carrying multiple meanings could signify all those meanings at the same time. This multiple application includes both literal and metaphorical, similar and divergent meanings. For example, in the following verse: "Seest thou not that to Allah bow down in worship all things that are in the heavens and on earth, the sun, the moon, the stars; the hills, the trees, the animals; and a great number among mankind?" (22:18).

In the above verse, the word *sujūd* (prostration) literally means placing one's forehead on earth, while it metaphorically means glorifying Allah. In this verse, both literal as well as metaphorical meanings are simultaneously applicable.

Another example of multiple literal and metaphorical meanings intended at the same time by one word is the verse "and stretch forth their hands and their tongues against you for evil" (60:2).

Here "extending the hands" literally means extending them for the purpose of beating and looting. While "extending the tongues" means not restraining from foul speech. And in this verse, this one word has been employed in both literal and metaphorical meanings at the same time.

And the example of using a composition of words in both ways is the verse "Woe to those that deal in fraud" (83:1). These words are at once information and a prayer against these evil mongers.

---

1 Mas'ūd bin 'Umar al-Taftāzānī, *Sharḥ al-Talwīh 'alā al-Tawḍīḥ* (n.p.: Dār al-'Ahd al-Jadīd li al-Ṭibā'ah, n.d.), 1: 67.

CHAPTER TEN

ON THE INIMITABILITY OF THE QUR'ĀN

There is no aim more formidable and challenging for the scholars of the Qur'ān than studying the subject of the inimitability of the Qur'ān. This topic has to this day engaged the attention of the Masters of Arabic Rhetoric. The science of Rhetoric has been a field of study in which many works were written in the past dealing with significant aspects of the inimitability of the Qur'ān. These works also tried to distinguish between literal and metaphorical aspects of Rhetoric. However, this area of study treated all features of the rhetorical qualities of Arabic language so as to define the criteria for criticism and evaluation of all the products of this language. It was through this procedure that the writers on the subject attempted to demonstrate the superiority of the Qur'ān over all forms of rhetorical expression. This work was done with the aid of evidence from the Qur'ān that encompassed all those features of rhetorical perfection that were never seen together in any other piece of language produced by the masters of Arabic rhetoric. That was why all early and later generations failed to produce a single piece similar to any specimen in the Qur'ān.

Abū Ya'qūb al-Sakkākī says, in his work *al-Miftāḥ*, "it should be noted that I have set forth in this science such principles as would fascinate everyone who builds upon them his ideas and every master of the field of Rhetoric will then acknowledge his expertise in it."[1] He goes on to say "...then after you have acquired a taste for it and perused the language of the Almighty, such things will reveal themselves to

1 Yūsuf bin Abī Bakr Muḥammad bin 'Alī al-Sakkākī, *Miftāḥ al-'Ulūm*, 300.

you that will enhance your honor and prestige. You will then be able to unveil the miraculous aspects of this Book."[1]

In this introduction our endeavor will be confined to showing only some glimpses of the miraculous qualities of the Qur'ān. This much would enable you to appreciate the miraculous nature of the Divine Parole.

We do not intend to exhaust the arguments for the miraculousness of the Qur'ān as reflected in its individual verses and chapters. For this subject has been adequately treated in the relevant works that contain all the general ideas and the particulars of the subject.

The brief exposition that we shall attempt here will enable the reader to understand the rhetorical qualities and literary subtleties of the Qur'ān, qualities that greatly enriched and expanded the Arabic language and its literary tradition. The reader will be able to appreciate in sum how the Qur'ān unlocked human understanding and unveiled new vistas to the human mind; how it conquered countries and kingdoms and how it elevated the Arabs' literary standards to the highest peaks, unreached by any other literary tradition of human culture or society. Many scholars who pursued this subject in the past have confused the two aspects, namely the impact of the Qur'ān on Arabic language and literature as a whole and the linguistic and literary miracle of the Qur'ān. The latter, in our view, constitutes an essential part of any introduction to the science of *tafsīr*. You will find in this introduction some of those principles and insights that escaped notice by many past scholars dealing with the miraculous aspect of the Qur'ān like al-Bāqillānī, al-Rummānī, 'Abd al-Qāhir, al-Khaṭṭābī, Qāḍī 'Iyaḍ and al-Sakkākī. No scholar of *tafsīr* can do justice to his vocation unless he includes in his exegetical notes on the meanings and nuances of the Qur'ānic verses, the subtleties of the rhetorics of the Qur'ān as much as his capacity enables him to do so. Therefore, each scholar of *tafsīr* is in need of elaborating modes of Arabic usage and rhetorical qualities

1 Ibid., 301.

that flow in the Qur'ānic stream and which matchlessly surpass all other products of human language. Failing to take care of this essential aspect of *tafsīr* will render the author incompetent and he will then be reduced to the status of a mere translator.

It is, nevertheless, regrettable to find many works on *tafsīr* lacking interest in this important aspect, with the exception of certain basic works in the field. Some of their authors have paid only scant attention to it, like Abū Isḥāq al-Zujāj in *Ma'ānī al-Qur'ān*, and 'Abd al-Ḥaqq bin 'Aṭiyyah al-Andalūsī in *al-Muḥarrir al-Wajīz*. On the other hand, there are some authors who have adequately treated this aspect in their works. The most prominent example of the latter category is Jār Allāh al-Zamakhsharī in his famous work *al-Kashshāf*.

The only group of scholars who could be excused on this lapse are the ones who have followed a particular aspect of *tafsīr* in their works, like those that deal with the legal study of the Qur'ān. Nonetheless, even some of these scholars could not overlook this highly precious substance in the Qur'ān like Ismā'īl bin Isḥāq al-Mālikī in his *Aḥkām al-Qur'ān*.

Further, this keen concern to establish and elaborate the miraculous nature of the Qur'ān has sprung from a foundational principle of Islam namely, that the Qur'ān is the greatest and the ever-abiding miracle given to the Prophet of Islam (peace be upon him). For it is this miracle whereby the Prophet (peace be upon him) had given an open challenge to his opponents. The Qur'ān says: "Ye they say: 'Why are not Signs sent down to him from his Lord?' Say: 'The signs are indeed with Allah: and I am indeed a clear Warner. And is it not enough for them that we have sent down to thee the Book which is rehearsed to them?'" (29:50-51).

Imām Abū Bakr al-Bāqillānī took up the task of establishing the argument for this doctrine in his work *I'jāz al-Qur'ān* and has dealt with this theme in detail. In sum, the prophethood of our Prophet (peace be upon him) has been founded on the Qur'ānic miracle though it was subsequently supplemented and reinforced by many other miracles. However, these latter miracles appeared in particular conditions and circumstances of space and time and they took place with particular people. Some of them were transmitted by overwhelming narrations while others were reported by particular individuals. The Qur'ān, on the contrary, has been a universal miracle. The testimony of truth has been attached to it since its appearance and shall remain so until the end of this world.

Its miraculous nature is established by the fact that people of the first era of Islam failed to produce a specimen similar to it; and this fact dispenses with a renewed reflection; and also the consistent failure of the subsequent eras to do so lends further evidence to prove its inimitability. The fact of this failure on the part of the opponents of the Qur'ān, has been continuously proven not only by the clear and open proclamation of the Qur'ān but also by the established record of history. The Qur'ān frequently records the historical evidence of the utter failure of its early auditors to meet its challenge to produce a single chapter similar to the Qur'ān. This fact constitutes a living testimony for the miraculous nature of the Qur'ān not only for those people who witnessed the revelation, but also for subsequent generations. In fact the Qur'ān went further and declared that the opponents shall never succeed in meeting this challenge. Thus both the challenge of the Qur'ān and the failure of people to meet this challenge are supported by overwhelming evidence of history. The Qur'ān says "And if ye are in doubt as to what We have revealed from time to time to Our servant, then produce a Sura like thereunto; and call your witnesses or helpers (If there are any) besides Allah, if your (doubts) are true But if ye cannot – and of a surety ye cannot – then fear the Fire" (2:23-24), "Or do they say, 'he forged it'? say: 'bring then a Sura like unto it, and call (to your aid) anyone you can besides Allah, if it be ye speak the truth'" (10:38) and it says: "Or they may say, 'He forged it,' say, 'bring ye then ten suras forged, like unto it, and call (to your aid) whomsoever ye can, other than Allah! If ye speak the truth If then they (your false gods) answer not your (call), know ye that this revelation is sent down (replete) with the knowledge of Allah, and that there is no god but He'" (11:13-14).

The continuous silence of all opponents and the repeated challenge in the Qur'ān, despite all reasons for the enemies of Islam to meet the challenge posed to them, is an incontrovertible and established fact of history.

The scholars of Islam have had a slight difference of opinion regarding the nature of the failure of people to produce a specimen similar to the Qur'ān. A small minority of scholars – mostly belonging to the *Mu'tazilah* school – hold that since Allah deprived people of the ability to imitate the Qur'ān, they failed to do so. This view has been known as *ṣarfah* (disabling).[1] However, the majority of scholars hold that since the Qur'ān was at such a height of eloquence and rhetorical perfection as was unattainable by all the masters of Arabic eloquence and rhetorical communication, they failed to produce anything similar to one single chapter of the Qur'ān.[2] We have in our present work adopted this latter view for obvious reasons.

It is significant to note that the Qur'ān challenges its opponents to produce a single chapter similar to it even though that chapter were short. It does not challenge them to produce a certain number of verses. The reason is that many features of the rhetoric are related to the total symmetry of speech. The beginning and end of a chapter is composed in such a pattern as could fulfill the purposes for which the speech is intended. Between the beginning and the end of a coherent and compact chapter there is to be found a transition from the main theme of the chapter to a sub-theme and then a return to the main theme. There are also found within the body of a single chapter the arts of pauses, brevity and elaboration, digression and intervening sentences. That is why

---

1 Mas'ūd bin 'Umar al-Taftāzānī, *Sharḥ al-Maqāṣid*, 'Abd al-Raḥmān 'Umayrah (Beirut: 'Ālam al-Kutub, 1419/1998), 6: 28.

2 Ibid.

Sharaf al-Dīn al-Ṭībī has regarded this fact as the reason for the Qur'ānic challenge to produce a chapter rather than any number of individual verses.

Since the detailed statement of all the aspects of the inimitability of the Qur'ān is something beyond the capacity of an individual, it is necessary to set forth its main ingredients. In our view, these ingredients are three.

(1) It has reached the utmost heights of rhetorical communication that is possible in Arabic language. It has such a symmetry of speech that contains in its folds subtle meanings and nuances far beyond the original semantics of Arabic. Such linguistic variety of style and richness of meaning could not be attained by the masters of rhetoric among the Arabs, neither in their prose nor poetry.

(2) The innovations introduced by the Qur'ān in the composition of speech and construction of sentences that were unfamiliar in the stylistics of the Arabs. Yet all these innovations have been made within the regular system of the language.

(3) It has invested its language with such an invaluable wealth of profound wisdom and allusions to intellectual and scientific realities that were unattained to the minds of men at the time of the revelation of the Qur'ān and during the subsequent periods. This latter aspect of the miracle was something that escaped notice of such scholars as Abū Bakr al-Bāqillānī and Qāḍī 'Iyāḍ.

Some scholars have added a fourth aspect of inimitability: its containing such reports about unseen matters that prove its Divine authorship. What Qāḍī 'Iyāḍ has counted as the fourth aspect of inimitability could also be included in this category: that it reports about the past generations such events that only few exceptional men of knowledge among the people of the Book could have known and that too only in part.[1] This aspect is indeed miraculous for the Arabs though it might not be so for the Jews and the Christians.

Therefore, the miraculous character of the Qur'ān is relevant to the Arabs, particularly from the first two aspects mentioned above. Because it is beyond imitation for the masters of eloquence and oratory among the Arabs in a direct way. For the common Arabs, it is a miracle to them in an indirect way through their knowledge of the fact that the opponents have failed to imitate it despite compelling causes for them to do so. This for them provides sufficient evidence that imitating this Book was beyond the capacity of all contestants. At the same time, it provides argument to the rest of humanity in favor of the truthfulness of the Prophet (peace be upon him) to whom this Book was revealed because the historical evidence of the failure of the Arabs is overwhelming. In this way, for the Arab people witnessing the Revelation, it is a miracle in terms of detailed argument furnished to them and for the rest of mankind, its miraculous nature is established on the whole.

Also those who learn the language of the Arabs and become well-versed in its literary and linguistic standards by long study and practice, are to be included among the Arabs in this regard. Because, as al-Sakkākī remarked, such non-Arabs could attain the ability to know in detail the reasons for which the Arabs who were challenged to imitate the Qur'ān, failed to do so.[2]

In short, everyone can know the failure of the early Arabs to meet the challenge of the Qur'ān, on the basis of historical evidence whether he is an Arab or non-Arab, and whether he lived in that era or in any other era. While the Arab people who witnessed the revelation as well as those who attain sufficient linguistic competence and literary skill

1 'Ayyāḍ (sic) bin Mūsā al-Yaḥṣubī, *Kitāb al-Shifā' bi Ta'rīf Ḥuqūq al-Muṣṭafā*, Kamāl Basyūnī Zaghlūl al-Miṣrī, ed., 3rd ed. (Beirut: Mu'assasat al-Kutub al-Thaqāfiyyah, n.d.), 1: 205-07.

2 Yūsuf bin Abī Bakr Muḥammad bin 'Alī al-Sakkākī, *Miftāḥ al-'Ulūm*, 248.

among the non-Arabs could appreciate the inimitability of the Qur'ān in greater depth in a direct way.

Also, the Qur'ān is a miracle from a third aspect for the entire mankind. It has enjoyed this status throughout history. The scholars of Islam have held that "the Qur'ān is a continuous miracle in that the men of reason could perceive its miraculous character even though they might not belong to the Arab community. They can do so by translating its legal, rational, scientific and ethical principles and precepts. Thus, it provides a detailed understanding of its miraculous nature to those who acquire knowledge of these principles and a brief perception of it is available to all those who receive a testimony of it from the former". This, in a nutshell, is the substance in terms of which we determine the miraculous character of the Qur'ān.

The first aspect of the Qur'ān's inimitability is based on the fact that it reaches the highest degree of eloquence and rhetorical excellence. This highest degree has been termed by the scholars of Islam as the miraculous degree. The Arabs were known for their mutual envy on the degree of eloquence and rhetorical communication that anyone among them attained. The masters of rhetoric and literary style have founded specific disciplines for explaining these linguistic attainments. They have taken up this task by comparing the Qur'ānic forms of rhetoric and the highest masterpieces of eloquence preserved among the Arabs. Scholars like Abū Bakr al-Bāqillānī, Abū Hilāl al-'Askarī, 'Abd al-Qāhir al-Jurjānī, al-Sakkākī and Ibn al-Athīr came forward with their monumental works in the field. They presented critical comparison between the Qur'ānic art of rhetorical expression and the celebrated specimens of Arabs' literary heritage. These discussions of Muslim scholars have marshaled sufficiently convincing evidence to establish the linguistic and literary miracle of the Qur'ān.

However, a brief exposition of this subject as the present one cannot encompass all aspects of this theme due to its varied and abundant forms and manifestations. It would, therefore, suffice to refer to the main sources for a detailed knowledge of the subject. These sources include: *Dalā'il al-I'jāz* by al-Jurjānī and *Asrār al-Balāghah* by the same author and part three and the subsequent chapters of *Miftāḥ al-'Ulūm* by al-Sakkākī and such other works. At the same time, for a detailed description of the miraculous features of the Qur'ānic verses, we direct the readers' attention to those works of *tafsīr* that had been written specifically for this purpose. The foremost among these works is *al-Kashshāf* by 'Allāmah al-Zamakhsharī. On our part, we will also be referring to these aspects in our present work on *tafsīr*. However, we would like to mention in this introduction certain basic principles relating to some aspects of the inimitability of the Qur'ān, aspects that were either overlooked by the early scholars or were touched upon by them only briefly.

For a brief argument to prove the miraculous status of the Qur'ān, it is sufficient to note that Allah addressed an open challenge to all the masters of Arabic Rhetoric to produce a single chapter like that of the Qur'ān, still none of them came forward to take up the task. In this way they demonstrated an acknowledgement of the truth and saved themselves from exposure to defeat and disgrace. This was despite the fact that these people had extraordinary ability in the art of expression – both in verse and prose and in themes of hope and fear alike – and they were distinguished for possessing sound mind, strong memory, eloquence of speech and clarity of expression. Therefore, articulating any kind of ideas, including even the most problematic themes was not difficult for them given their exceptional talents.

Qāḍī 'Iyāḍ says in his work *al-Shifā'* "the Prophet (peace be upon him) continued to strike them with the challenge rebuking them sternly, condemning their vision and damning their heroes and yet they utterly failed to confront him or attempt any imitation of this miracle. Instead they deceived themselves by denying his truthfulness and leveling false allegations against him. Sometimes, they said: 'this is a magic that could be overcome', 'this is a continuous magic', 'this is an open fabrication!', 'these are only myths of the ancient people'; In response to them, Allah said: 'if you cannot (imitate this Book) and you shall never be able to imitate ...'; still these people could never do anything to vindicate themselves, nor acquired any capacity to do anything."[1]

If anyone was stupid enough to attempt this like Musaylamah, his stupidity was exposed to all. And when Walīd bin Mughīrah heard the verse "Allah commands justice and the doing of good" (16:90), he remarked "there is a sweetness in this and a splendor. Its lower portion is fertile and its higher side fruit-yielding. It is certainly not a human speech."[2] Abū 'Ubaydah says that a Bedouin heard someone reciting the verse: "Therefore expound openly what thou art commanded" (15:94), and he immediately fell prostrated saying "I have prostrated to its eloquence."[3] The impactful part in the sentence is the word *iṣda'* which expresses the sense of preaching candidly, openly and courageously. And the words "what you are commanded" are effective for their brevity and comprehensiveness.

Another man is reported to have heard someone reciting the words of the Qur'ān: "Now when they saw no hope of his (yielding), they held a conference in private" (12:80), he exclaimed: "I testify that no human is capable of such speech."[4]

Further, that the Prophet (peace be upon him) challenged his Arab opponents with the miracle of the Qur'ān and the Arabs failed in their opposition is a fact that is essentially established in brief and which the scholars of rhetoric have labored to elaborate. Al-Sakkākī says in *al-Miftāḥ*:

You should bear in mind that the miraculous nature of the Qur'ān is a marvelous trait, a trait that could be felt but not described. It is like the balance and harmony of human physique. It could be felt but not described. Or we could say that it is like human charm. The real way of feeling the miracle in my opinion is taste, nothing else. The way of acquiring this taste is to put oneself in the service of the twain disciplines of Rhetorics and Stylistics. No doubt, however, that there are certain

---

1 'Ayyāḍ (sic) bin Mūsā al-Yaḥṣubī, *Kitāb al-Shifā' bi Ta'rīf Ḥuqūq al-Muṣṭafā*, 1: 198-99.

2 Ibid., 1: 199.

3 Ibid.

4 Ibid., 1: 199-200.

aspects of rhetoric that remain somewhat hidden until veils are removed from them and they become clear to you. As to the real essence of the miraculous, it defies description.[1]

In his comments on the remarks of al-Sakkākī, al-Taftāzānī says: "what he means to say is that whatever we can grasp by our intellects, we could also express it quite often. But the matter of miracle is different. Because we definitely know from the speech of Allah that this speech was not imitable for humans and that it was unlike the language of any Arab master of eloquence. Even though the words of the Qur'ān are the same as the words of the Arabs' language and so are its forms of constructions. It is like a speech about which we know definitely that it has a balanced form of construction rather than any other. Also it is like our knowing someone to be balanced in the physical proportion while others to be like him or less than him in that respect. But over and above this harmony and proportion, there is a peculiar charm in him which we cannot clearly know what it is though we could feel it all right."[2]

Likewise, the way of appreciating the miraculous qualities of the Qur'ān, according to al-Sakkākī, is nothing but taste (*dhawq*).

Dhawq is a special kind of cognitive power and aesthetic sensibility that is specially gifted to someone to perceive the subtleties of language and its hidden beauties.

If this taste has been bestowed upon someone by nature then this is the real locus of it. But if someone tries to acquire it, then there is no way to obtain it other than engaging oneself with the disciplines of Rhetoric and Stylistics and long practice and involvement with them. However, if somebody combines his natural taste with a long active association with them, then no ambition is higher than this. This is indeed the height of human attainment.

---

1 Yūsuf bin Abī Bakr Muḥammad bin 'Alī al-Sakkākī, *Miftāḥ al-'Ulūm*, 416.

2 For this debate see al-Taftāzānī's *Sharḥ al-Maqāṣid*, Ibrāhīm Shams al-Dīn (introduction and notes) (Beirut: Dār al-Kutub al-'Ilmiyyah, 2010), 3/288 ff. (Ed.)

Therefore, the miraculous aspect of the Qur'ān belongs to the realm of rhetorics and stylistics. It is not at all due to so-called *ṣarfah* as Naẓẓam and a group of *mu'tazila* have opined. *Ṣarfah*, according to them, means that Allah has averted the Arabs from opposing the Qur'ān and deprived them of the ability to produce a specimen of its style. Nor does its miraculousness come from adopting a style different from the one practiced by the Arabs in their poetics, orations and epistles as contented by another group of scholars. According to this latter group, this unique style of the Qur'ān was particularly reflected in the openings and endings of its chapters and verses like the words: *yu'minūn yunfiqūn* and *ya'lamūn*. Nor is this miracle exhibited by its being immune from contradictions[1] despite its long discourses as pointed out by Sayyid Jurjānī.[2] Nor is it displayed in its expressing news of the unseen. All these notions are baseless. Al-Jurjānī has enumerated these five opinions and then said "These five are the opinions about the miraculous aspects of the Qur'ān and there is no sixth opinion about it."[3]

What Sayyid Jurjānī wanted to emphasize was that though the miracle itself was beyond human understanding, one could still discover aspects of rhetorical excellence in terms of which it is possible to appreciate the inimitability of the Qur'ān.[4]

Among the rhetorical qualities that the Qur'ān is replete with is the beauty of distribution of speech into clear thematic units like in the chapter "Opening". It has been distributed into seven clearly distinguishable units.

These qualities include the use of alliteration in so many verses like "Others they turn away from it, and themselves they keep away" (6:26). Alliteration is regarded an important feature of the beauty of speech.

Now we would like to cite below some of those aspects of the inimitability to which our knowledge has guided us.

---

1 Ibid., 291. (Ed.).

2 Al-Sayyad al-Sharīf 'Alī bin Muḥammad bin 'Alī al-Jurjānī, *al-Miṣbāḥ fī Sharḥ al-Miftāḥ*, 714.

3 Ibid.

4 Ibid., 713-14.

We notice among the skills of effective communication the art of digression. The latter means shifting the speech from first to second and third persons. This shift in itself is reckoned among the fine traits of an eloquent speech. The famous master of linguistics Ibn Jinnī has called it the "boldness of Arabic", since this transition renews the listener's interest.[1] But if this digression is further augmented by a subtle compatibility requiring the transition, then this is regarded a great rhetorical virtue. The Arab masters of eloquence recognized it as a precious quality of speech. In the Qur'ān, we find countless examples of this artful skill of transition along with an accurate compatibility.

Similarly, simile and metaphor have been regarded as instruments of high value in the sphere of rhetoric. It is through these means of literary acumen that the foremost poet of Arabia, Imru' al-Qays, excelled his peers and rose to renown in pre-Islamic era. There appeared such forms of simile and metaphor in the Qur'ān that rendered the Arabs unable to emulate like "and the hair of my head doth glisten with grey" (19:4), "and lower to them the wing of humility" (17:24), "And a Sign for them is the Night: We withdraw therefrom the Day" (36:37) and "swallow up thy water" (11:44) and other marvelous forms of linguistic embellishment.

Notice the wonderful illustration in the following verse: "Does any of you wish that he should have a garden with date-palms and vines under which flow streams" (2:266).

This verse provides an example of covering all dimensions of the total beauty of simile to express the most intense regret over the loss.

---

1 See, Abū al-Fatḥ 'Uthmān bin Jinnī, *al-Khaṣā'iṣ*, 2: 360. It is to be noted, however, that Ibn Jinnī does not count *al-Iltifāt* among the elements of *Shujā'at al-'Arabiyyah* in *Bāb fī Shujā'at al-'Arabiyyah*, nor does he call it *Shujā'at al-'Arabiyyah* elsewhere in his book. M. Islam.
While it is actually Ibn Athīr who develops Ibn Jinnī's idea of *Shujā'at al-'Arabiyyah* to include *Iltifāt*, in his *Baqiyyat al-khāṭiriyyāt*, Ibn Jinnī seems to suggest that Iltifāt is a part of *Taṣarruf* (manipulation), which according to him is included in the "boldness of Arabic". See Ibn Jinnī, *Baqiyyat al-khāṭiriyyāt*, Muḥammad Aḥmad al-Dālī (ed.) Maṭbū'āt Majma' al-Lughah al-'Arabiyyah (Damascus: Maṭba'at al-Ṣabāḥ, 1992), 25-26. (Ed).

There is another example of a perfect simile in the verse: "The Parable of His Light is as if there were a Niche and within it a Lamp: the Lamp enclosed in Glass: the glass as it were a brilliant star: Lit from a blessed Tree, an Olive, neither of the east nor of the west, whose oil is well-nigh luminous" (24:35).

In this verse such attributes and conditions have been mentioned that supply an enhanced explanation of the intensity of light mentioned here. These devices add to the beauty of that for which the simile has been employed. And all these things greatly augment the forceful communication by means of this simile.

The Qur'ānic composition is based on abundance of meaning and plurality of connotation. The sentences in the Qur'ān convey, on the one hand, all the conventional connotations shared by the regular Arabic usage, and, on the other hand, over and above that, they supply additional rhetorical connotations that are in sum shared by the language of the masters of eloquence though the latter by no means attain its levels of rhetorical communication.

There is another kind of connotation supplied by the words of the Qur'ān. We could call it enfolded connotation. The latter is the presumed sense conveyed by the Qur'ānic words implicitly on the basis of a certain circumstantial factor requiring that presumed sense. This kind of connotation is rarely found in the language of the Arab masters of rhetoric. However, it is present in abundance in the Qur'ān. In this category, a certain statement, relative clause or adjective is presumed within the body of the language construction without being expressly mentioned.

There is also a particular connotation that is conveyed by the position of a sentence in relation to its *infra* and *supra*. For example, some sentence could assume the status of a cause for the foregoing statement or an emendation for it or could take the place of an answer to a preceding question or an insinuation to something etc. This type of connotation is seldom found in the parole of the Arabs because of the limited scope of their themes. However, since the Qur'ān is a Book of reminder and recital, its infinitude explains this vast expanse of meaning and plurality of purpose.

An example of the above category is the verse of the Qur'ān: "Allah created the heavens and the earth for just ends, and in order that each soul may find the recompense of what it has earned, and none of them be wronged" (45:22) which comes after the verse: "What! Do those who seek after evil ways think that We shall hold them equal with those who believe and do righteous deeds, that equal will be their life and their death? Ill is the judgment that they make" (45:21).

The former contains a sense of teaching and reminder in view of its construction. And the preceding verse invests it with an added sense of an argument to support the foregoing statement.

Also, the order maintained between various ingredients of sentences, some of which precede while the other succeed or is placed in the middle, invests the language of the Qur'ān with marvelous subtleties of meanings and nuances that are beyond human capacity to count. We shall also be drawing the readers' attention to this aspect from time to time when the occasion so requires.

Another point which deserves notice is that catering for the requirement of the situation and composing the speech with rhetorical qualities is one of the chief ingredients of an eloquent speech and this ingredient occupies an important place in the inimitability of the Qur'ān. At times, a verse of the Qur'ān is invested with certain qualities. And the scholar of *tafsīr* asks himself the reasons and the requirements that could explain to him their significance. He looks for those reasons but brings up an explanation which appears artificial or concocted. This happens because he does not pay attention except to the position of words in the verse. While actually the requirement of that particular composition of phrase should be sought in the situation in which that verse has been revealed. An example of this is to be found in the verse: "They are the Party of the Evil One. Truly, it is the Party of the Evil

One that will perish" (58:19) followed by the verse: "They are the Party of Allah. Truly it is the Party of Allah that will achieve Felicity" (58:22).

In these verses, the word of caution: *alā* occurring in the beginning of the two verses appears somewhat difficult to explain. The scholar of *tafsīr* seeks an explanation and tries to understand the requirement for this word of caution and he explains it in a general way. For instance, he would say "this word of caution has been inserted here to underline the importance of the news conveyed in these verses." However, when we take notice of the fact that these two verses were revealed in the presence of the believers and the hypocrites we could clearly explain the significance of bringing this word of caution. It has been brought in the first verse to awaken both the groups of believers and hypocrites. For the hypocrites, the message is "we know your hidden selves." This is because these people pretended to the believers that they were not in Satan's party since they had adopted an appearance of the believers. As to the second group namely, the believers, the message conveyed to them is "exercise caution against these people and remain awake to their nature. For those who befriend your enemies are also your own enemies because they belong to Satan's party. And since Satan is Allah's enemy, he is your enemy too."

Similarly, bringing the word of caution in the second verse is to awaken these hypocrites to the virtues of the believers so that they might turn away from their hypocrisy. At the same time, this verse strikes a note of caution to the believers by saying to them: "there are around you a group of people who do not belong to Allah's party and they are not going to attain to salvation. So beware of them."

The source of this kind of inimitability is what the scholars of rhetoric call the subtle points of rhetoric. The Arab masters of this field used to compete with each other in enriching their language with these points. This was regarded the main touchstone for judging the standards of eloquence among them. When these people heard the Qur'ān, they comprehended the richness of the Qur'ān in this respect and realized that this richness was far beyond their linguistic competence and literary skill. I think these people must have thought of seeking assistance from each other in countering this challenge of the Qur'ān only to recognize their failure in this venture because they were well aware of their limitations as well as the supernatural level of the Qur'ān in this sphere. Their joint concern and collective deliberation, however, failed to enable them to confront this miracle.

It must have been after the utter failure of their joint effort to compete with the eloquent style of the Qur'ān that they became aware of their inability and the inimitability of the Qur'ān. It was then that the Qur'ān recorded the fact that these people had failed in their attempt individually as well as collectively, as the Qur'ān emphatically declared: "they could not produce the like thereof, even if they backed up each other with help and support" (17:88).

The above evidence remains the most important foundation of the miraculous status of the Qur'ān, a status that fully characterizes even its shortest chapter.

In the matter of the Qur'ān's inimitability, there is another aspect worthy of note. This aspect is related to the elegance of each individual word of the Qur'ān that in consonance with other words in perfect harmony and symmetry of composition singularly creates an inimitable style. For this is a composition that is fully immune from heaviness of intonation and hardness of pronunciation in both its individual words and its composition. Imām Fakhr al-Dīn Rāzi says in his *Mafātīḥ al-Ghayb* "the beauty of words is not abandoned even in a speech of wisdom. Every speech has a body, that is its words, and a soul which is its meaning. Like a human being whose soul has been enlightened with knowledge, so his body ought to be enlightened by cleanliness. Similar is the nature of speech. At times, even a phrase of wisdom remains ineffective due to feebleness of its words."[1]

1 Al-Fakhr al-Rāzī, *al-Tafsīr al-Kabīr*, 28: 206.

The Arab poets and orators often fell prey to the use of words or dialects that were hard for the tongue to utter. This hardness was felt both in individual words and in the combination of words. This is what has been termed in the science of eloquence as dissonance among the letters of one word or among words in a certain combination like: *mustashzirāt* and *al-Kanahbal*, words employed by Imru' al-Qāys in his famous Ode. Similarly, *safannajah* and *al-Khafaydad*, words occurring in the Ode of another famous Poet of pre-Islamic Arabia, namely Ṭarafah bin al-'Abd. A typical example of dissonance in a combination of words is the line attributed to an unknown poet:

وقبر حفر بمكان قفر   وليس قرب قبر حرب قبر

(Ḥarb's grave lies at a deserted place; and there is not found any other grave beside Ḥarb's) *Wa laysa qurba qabri Ḥarbin qabrū*. However, the Qur'ān is totally immune from all these forms of dissonance in letters and disharmony in words. This is despite the fact that it treats a variety of themes requiring abundant use of varied vocabulary.

In short, the Qur'ān was revealed with the best of dialects and its vocabulary is free from any cumbersome words or heavy expressions in order to facilitate its reception by the auditors. The Qur'ān itself points to this fact in the refrain "And We have indeed made the Qur'an easy to understand and remember: then is there any that will receive admonition?" (54:17).

In this respect, it should be noted that the words of the Qur'ān are characterized by clarity and candidness. The Qur'ān chooses to express the intended meaning in the words that are nearest to conveying that meaning. At the same time, these words are also the most comprehensive in that they encompass all the varieties of significations and nuances that are included in the given message. Thus there is no word that falls short of any aspect of the meanings intended in the composition of words. Also it is worth noting that despite intending a vast spectrum of meanings, the words of the Qur'ān preserve their original linguistic connotations. An example of this is the use of the word *ḥard* (determination, strong resolve) in the verse "And they opened the morning, strong in an (unjust) resolve" (68:25). Here this word *ḥard* and all its connotations are the most fitting for this occasion. At the same time, the Qur'ān uses words in their metaphorical and figurative senses and places indicators for this use within the context itself, so that the speech is free from any confusion.

Where the context requires any manipulation (*taṣarruf*) in the construction to convey the meaning intended by a word, then this is done through impregnating the construction with the extended meaning (*taḍmīn*). The latter is a frequently employed linguistic device in the Qur'ān. An example of this device is the verse: "And the (Unbelievers) must indeed have passed by the town on which was rained a shower of evil" (25:40).

The verb *ataw* has been brought here implying the sense "they passed by ...." That is why it has been followed by the preposition *'alā* before the object: *al-qaryah*. Now, a composition such as this has yielded an extended sense of taking lesson from the fate of the inhabitants of this particular town (which they had passed). Any other construction could not have delivered the meaning of passing by the ruins of a town and taking lesson from the ill-fated end of its inhabitants. And all these devices, far from violating the established stylistic standards of eloquence, are reckoned among its subtle merits and precious qualities. These qualities are rare even in the language of the elect masters of eloquence because of the obvious limitations of human intelligence to encompass all these considerations at once.

The second aspect is related to the innovations introduced by the Qur'ān in manipulating with variety of style in presenting its eloquent speech. This is an aspect that had been generally overlooked in the science of Rhetoric. The literary lore of the Arabs had been divided into prose and poetry. The prose mainly consisted of orations and rhymes of the soothsayers. The producers of these genres – despite their competition in innovating new meanings and varied compositions in poetry – mainly followed more or less the same or similar patterns in both poetry and prose. They almost adhered to the conventional pattern that they had been familiar with in their tradition. So much so that a poet almost invariably followed the same mode for the beginning of an ode. There are so many odes that start with the words: *bānat Su'ād* as we find in the odes of Nābighah and Ka'b bin Zuhayr.

Similar was the case in their orations that followed one tone and style as is reflected in the orations of Saḥbān and Quss bin Sā'idah. As to the rhymes of soothsayers, these had been peculiar for brevity of phrases and unfamiliar words. However, the predominant medium of the Arabs' language had been poetry, while oratory was a rare production due to the rarity of its occasions. To 'Umar bin al-Khaṭṭāb (may God be pleased with him) is attributed the statement "poetry was the utmost fund of knowledge possessed by these people. To them no other knowledge was more authentic."[1] Therefore, the main competition of eloquence was witnessed in the field of versified expressions. When the Qur'ān came, it was neither poetry nor the rhymed prose typical of the soothsayers. Rather it was nearer to oration among the existing genres of prose. It introduced abundant innovations in style. Its style varied with variation in its themes. It introduced wonderful varieties of style and greatly enriched the language. Those familiar with the language of the Arabs were extremely enthused and enthralled with its stylistic wonders. That is why Walīd bin Mughīrah, after hearing the Prophet's recitation, made his famous remarks "by God he is no soothsayer, this language (of the Qur'ān) is not the typical rhyme of a soothsayer. We have known all the forms of poetry. He is no poet either."[2] Similar remarks have been attributed to Unays bin Junādat al-Ghifārī, the poet, and the brother of Abū Dharr, 'Utbah bin Rabī'ah and Naḍr bin Ḥārith.[3] Apparently when the polytheists could not find

1 Muḥammad bin Salām al-Jumaḥī, *Ṭabaqāt Fuḥūl al-Shu'arā'*, Maḥmūd Muḥammad Shākir, ed. (n.p.: Dār al-Ma'ārif li al-Ṭibā'ah wa al-Nash, n.d.), 22.

2 'Ayyāḍ (sic) bin Mūsā al-Yaḥṣubī, *Kitāb al-Shifā' bi Ta'rīf Ḥuqūq al-Muṣṭafā*, 1: 201.

3 Ibid., 1: 202.

any way of classifying the Qur'ān and placing it in any genre of their language, they linked it with the genre that seemed to them nearest to it, namely poetry. Because the common folk had been familiar with subtle ideas, norms of temperance and rationally convincing maxims that were the contents of their poetry. However, despite producing highest degree of Arabic eloquence, its treatment of extensive topics and varied themes and its being neither prose nor poetry, you will find the style of the Qur'ān remarkably lucid, running with smooth fluency; yet its eloquence is never interrupted and memorizing it is easier than poetry.

The Arabs had adopted the medium of poetry to immortalize their ideals and to represent their literary achievements. This was because the requirement for meters in poetry necessitated a training of the mind in the rhythm of words that created a certain symphony which in turn added to its fluency. That was why their prominent men of linguistic skill competed with each other in poetics. Still many of their great poets varied in the fluency of their verse with frequent omissions in this regard. However, such omissions were considered pardonable among them under poetic license. There could hardly be found among these Arab masters of eloquence anyone whose literary masterpiece of prose or verse, despite all its merit, could be free from cumbersome speech or other omissions that were regarded a deviation from the standards of eloquence. However, when the Qur'ān was revealed in their midst in simple and smooth prose, it surpassed all human literary productions in eloquence, fluency, harmony and total freedom from any cumbersome word or complicated phrase. The Arabs discovered in it a specimen of language that enjoyed all the smoothness and symphony characteristic of verse yet it was not verse. Thus, its being prose is an integral constituent of its miraculous status. The Qur'ān contained some forms of style that have been in vogue among the Arabs and, in addition, it introduced many innovative styles unknown to the Arabs. There was great Divine wisdom in this variation. First to show that this was from God. Because in every age, human literary genius shows itself only in one or two modes of style that are in vogue among them. Second, this intensified the challenge for them since none could assert that due to the novelty of its style, he could not compete with it and if it were in a familiar style, he might have attempted it.

Among the most prominent of Qur'ān's styles, in which it has followed a different course from the Arabs, is that it has adopted a mode of language that combines the themes of preaching and legislation. In appearance it seemed to its listeners that it was providing them instruction in those matters in which they needed guidance. In this respect, it appeared like the Arabs' orations. However, many deeper layers of meaning were discoverable in this discourse from which an insightful scholar could discern an abundance of ordinances and injunctions of legislative import and moral significance. There still remained many deeper levels of meaning in the same Parole about which it declared: "none knows their interpretation save God and those well-versed in knowledge" (3:7). This is because there still remain many allusions, in the meaning of its words, to certain universal truths, ultimate causes and paramount objectives of life and reality. Hence these deeper allusions are not accessible except to the elect few in this world.

Among the stylistic features of the Qur'ān is what I call *tafannun* i.e. artful transition from one mode to another such as intervening sentence, parallelism, supplementary statement, use of synonyms frequently to avoid the encumbrance of repeating the same words, and excessive digressions. The latter is regarded a grand art of language among the masters of eloquence and is found in abundance in the Qur'ān. This digression is followed by a reversion to the main theme so that the listener's interest and attentiveness is renewed. The most remarkable example of this art is found in the verse "Their similitude is that of a man who kindled a fire; when it lighted all around him, Allah took away their light and left them in utter darkness. So they could not see. Deaf, dumb, and blind, they will not return (to the path). Or (another similitude) is that of a rain-laden cloud from the sky: In it are zones of darkness, and thunder and lightning: They press their fingers in their ears to keep out the stunning thunder-clap, while they are in terror of death. But Allah is ever round the rejecters of Faith. The lightning all but snatches away their sight; every time the light (Helps) them, they walk therein, and when the darkness grows on them, they stand still. And if Allah willed, He could take away their faculty of hearing and seeing; for Allah hath power over all things." (2:17-20).

Many of the stylistic modes of the Qur'ān were those that were known but rarely attained in the poetry of the Arabs and in the orations of their paragons of eloquence. In the Qur'ānic art of employing varied stylistic patterns and a transition between these patterns, there is always a significant compatibility between the two. This creates a subtle innovative harmony between the former and the latter patterns of speech. The reader and the listener recognize the transition only when it occurs. Also this variety serves as an incentive to hearing and saves the hearer from monotone. This is because among the aims of the Qur'ān is to maximize its times of recitation. The Qur'ān says: "He knoweth that ye are unable to keep count thereof. So He hath turned to you (in mercy): read ye, therefore, of the Qur'ān as much as may be convenient for you" (73:20), the words "may be convenient" underscore its maximum recitation subject to convenience. And in the harmony of its parole and variety of themes, there is increasing convenience and an aid to excessive recitation. Abū Bakr bin Al-'Arabī says in his book *Sirāj al-Murīdīn*: "to find the mutual relation of Qur'ānic verses so that it appears like one word in meaning and well-organized in composition is a grand knowledge."[1]

In this respect, Shams al-Dīn Maḥmūd al-Aṣfahānī cites the following statement of Imām Fakhr al-Dīn Rāzī: "like the miracle of the Qur'ān in the elegance of its words and nobility of its meanings, it is also a miracle in its order and symmetry of words. Perhaps those

1 Muḥammad bin 'Abd Allāh al-Zarkashī, *al-Burhān fī 'Ulūm al-Qur'ān*, 1: 36.

who have said that the Qur'ān is miraculous due to its style have been pointing to this feature of the Qur'ān."[1]

The eloquence of language, however, is not confined to the composition of its words, but transcends it to the states of the mind and heart that this composition creates among its listeners.

It happens that when an eloquent speaker slightly pauses after a sentence, his silence increases listener's interest in what follows. For example in the verse: "Has the story of Moses reached thee? Behold, thy Lord did call to him in the sacred valley of Tuwa" (79:15-16), the pause at the name Mūsā creates in the listener a longing for the subsequent part of the parole about Mūsā. When this is followed by the words *idh nadāhu Rabbuhū* ... the statement is elaborated.

The author of *al-Kashshāf* says while explaining the verse: "Say: My Lord knoweth (every) word (spoken) in the heavens and on earth" (21:4):

it is not obligatory to bring the highest superlative on every occasion, but sometimes a lesser stress is given and at others a stronger one is considered more apt, just as at places a good expression is used and at others a still better one. This is done to create artistic variety of speech.[2]

Among the rhetorical features of the Qur'ān is included the expansion it made in the linguistic capital of Arabic. The prevailing literary lore of the Arabs mainly consisted of poetry, which formed the main source of their collective memory and circulated among them extensively. It followed a peculiar style in the choice of words and creative expression of meaning. Apart from poetry, other genres of the Arabic language seldom found a lasting place in the Arabs' memory. Their poetry had developed certain typical themes, the most famous and common of which were lyric, epic, satire, glory and pride. Apart from these genres of poetry, there were some others in which little amount of poetry was

1 Al-Fakhr al-Rāzī, *al-Tafsīr al-Kabīr*, 7: 138.

2 Maḥmūd bin 'Umar al-Zamakhsharī, *al-Kashshāf*, 4: 129.

produced like anecdotes and eulogy. Aside from poetry, their linguistic treasure also contained orations, proverbs and certain memorable dialogues. The orations were often forgotten after the end of the events on which these were delivered and their text had not been preserved for posterity. However, the impact of these orations lingered on in the memories of their listeners and they felt inspired by it in their conduct for a short while. However, this impact was partial and transitory. The proverbs were short words that aimed at deriving lessons on their particular occasions. The dialogues were mostly a routine of life, seldom inspiring any abiding interest due to their lack of importance. Some of these dialogues used to take place in public assemblies in the presence of kings and on the occasions of expressing self-pride and tribal glory. These public events, however, were rare occurrences and had limited immediate aims. Therefore, the memory of them soon faded from public consciousness. Further, these dialogues did not contain any substance, save expressions of self-glory and exaggerated amounts of self-praise. Nothing survived from them in public memory except witty repartee, an anecdote or some rhymed phrases like the dialogue of Imru' al-Qays with the chieftains of Banū Asad.

Against this cultural backdrop, the Qur'ān came up with a new literary mode that was at once quite rich and also appropriate for all minds. It touched by way of its artistic variety all the multifarious themes of life, giving to each theme the most appropriate concepts, vocabulary and dialect. It contained in its fold the elements of the genres of dialogue, oration, disputation, proverb, parables, depiction and narrative. Further, the elegance in its words, symmetry in its composition and organization on the innovative pattern of pauses that created a marvelous harmony in the ears of the listeners even without similarity of letters, as in rhymes, all these features made the Qur'ān easy to preserve in memory and fast to circulate among the tribes and clans. Over and above these features, the substance of the Qur'ān was pure truth rather than false exaggerations and imaginary self-glorifications so typical of the Arab lore. In this way, the Qur'ān exercised the force of truth and had a tremendous appeal to its listeners. This indeed was a spiritual influence, not that of words or meanings.

10.1. Innovations of the Qur'ān

The Qur'ān has introduced a number of creative innovations in its composition whereby it is distinguished from other specimens of Arabic language.

Among these innovations is that its peculiar mode is definitely opposed to the pattern of poetry as the early scholars of Islam have pointed out. I would like to add to this another feature, namely its being somewhat different from the style of oratory as well. It maintains the pattern of a book meant to be memorized and recited. And this is one of its miraculous features, since its whole composition has followed an innovative pattern quite different from previously established patterns of speech.

And I reckon among its distinctive innovations that it contained sentences signifying meaningful connotations written like sentences conveying intellectual and legislative content. Therefore, it neither makes any general statements that need specificity without specifying them, nor does it state such absolute norms that require particularity without particularization. On the other hand, the Arabs were not prone to use such an all-inclusive language due to their lack of conversance with treating rare conditions and unusual cases. An example of this is the verse: "Not equal are those believers who sit (at home) and receive no hurt, and those who strive and fight" (4:95) and the verse: "and who is more astray than one who follows his own lusts, devoid of guidance from Allah?" (28:50).

The latter verse contains the notion that some desire could also be meritorious if it is guided by Allah. Another example is the verse: "Verily Man is in loss. Except such as have Faith" (103:2-3).

These innovations include the manner of distributing the contents into distinct parts followed by a return to these parts one by one.

This was indeed a new mode hitherto unknown in Arabic language. The author of *al-Kashshāf* has also made a brief reference to it in his work.[1]

Another innovation of the Qur'ān is adopting a narrative style in the description of eschatological states of bliss in Paradise and chastisement in Hell, as also in the description of other stages of afterlife. This narration had a profound impact on the minds of Arabs, since narrative style was more or less non-existent in Arabic literature. When the Qur'ān came with a portrayal of the scenes of afterlife, the Arabs were greatly bewildered by this live description of afterlife like the one found in the chapter "Heights" starting with the words: "The Companions of the Garden will call out to the Companions of the Fire" (7:44), and in the chapter *al-Ḥadīd* that starts with the verse: "So a wall will be put up betwixt them, with a gate therein" (57:13).

Also related to this is the feature of the Qur'ān in narration that is represented by a manipulation of the style in accordance with the demands of the situation being depicted. In this manipulation, the Qur'ān recasts the composition of the narration so as to serve its rhetorical requirements rather than strictly conforming to the verbal version in which a past story might have come down. Thus when it narrates any non-Arabic statements, it molds them in a manner that reaches a miraculous eloquence in Arabic. Similarly, when it mentions Arabic statements, it casts the speech so as to conform to the Arabs' style of narrating the essence. It does not bind itself to mentioning the original words of the actors in the story. It rather articulates their essence. The Arabs used to exercise liberty of expression in the mentioning of statements so that the focus was on containing the meaning rather than a faithful reporting of words. Therefore, the inimitability that is established in the reported statements, is that of the Qur'ān, not that of the original statements. In the same way, the Qur'ān changes the names occurring in the stories to suit their position in

---

1 Maḥmūd bin 'Umar al-Zamakhsharī, *al-Kashshāf*, 1: 95.

speech in accordance with the demands of the eloquence like changing Shāwl to Ṭālūt and Tāraḥ to Āzar.

Included in the innovations of the Qur'ān is introduction of illustrative proverbs. In the literature of the Arabs also there had been frequent use of proverbs. A proverb was a symbolic description of certain incidents giving rise to some eloquent phrases that were said during those incidents or were said about them *ex post facto*. These phrases later became prevalent in the language as proverbs, and they alluded to those incidents. However, after the proverbs became frequently used for a long time, the original incidents that gave rise to them were forgotten and only their message clung to the minds at the time of their use in the language.

But the Qur'ān greatly elaborated and enriched the proverbs. It introduced innovation in their construction. For example see the following verses: "The parable of those who reject their Lord is that their works are as ashes, on which the wind blows furiously on a tempestuous day" (14:18), "if anyone assigns partners to Allah, is as if he had fallen from heaven and been snatched up by birds, or the wind had swooped (like a bird on its prey) and thrown him into a far-distant place" (22:31), "any others that they call upon besides Him hear them no more than if they were to stretch forth their hands for water to reach their mouths but it reaches them not"(13:14).

Another innovation is that the Qur'ān did not adhere to one style in all its chapters. The style varied in each chapter. Every chapter seems to have a new dialect and a fresh tone. Some of them follow intermittent rhymed pauses, while others do not display such a feature. Similar is the mode in the opening of the chapters. Some chapters open with a celebration of Divine praise. Some start with the address to the believers in the words: (O ye who believe). Others start with the words: Alif. Lām. Mīm. This is the Book.

This mode is proximate to what we call, in the art of prose-composition, an introduction. Still other chapters open with a direct agitation of the main theme like: "Those who reject Allah and hinder (men) from the Path of Allah, their deeds will Allah render astray (from their mark)" (47:1) and "A (declaration) of immunity from Allah and His Messenger" (9:1).

And by far the most creative of all innovations of the Qur'ān is brevity. This was the art in which the Arab masters of language competed with one another and vied for this accomplishment. The Qur'ān took this art to the highest summits. In addition to the brevity – as generally defined in the science of Rhetoric – there is in the Qur'ān another kind of remarkable brevity. It is the capacity of most of its verses to yield a plurality of meanings all of which fit well in the text without ambiguity or confusion. While some of these multiple meanings are such that all of them could be appreciated in combination. In other cases, if one meaning is admitted then others have to be excluded. This latter category serves to stimulate the minds and alert them to these extended meanings for the purpose of preaching and reminder inviting observance of something and refraining from something else. We have already referred to this latter category in Section IX of this introduction.

It should be borne in mind that but for the brevity in the Qur'ān, it was so concise and comprehensive. For otherwise this Book would have been many times bigger in volume to deliver all the expanses of meaningful ideas that are contained in its fold. The subtle meanings of the Revelation and its deep nuances in each of its themes are so profoundly compressed in its text that it is a formidable task for the most intelligent scholar to discern them. Yet there still remain certain aspects of these meanings inaccessible.

You will find in many Qur'ānic constructions, wonderful examples of ellipticism. However, you will never come across any example of ellipticism to which a clue is not available in the text itself or in the context. It is this unique feature of the Qur'ān whereby it supplies an abundance of meaning in a few words. Imām al-Zamakhsharī says in *al-Kashshāf* while dealing with the chapter *al-Muddaththir*: "ellipticism and brevity is the standard pattern of the Revelation."[1] One of the Patriarchs of Rome after hearing the verse "It is such as obey Allah and His Messenger, and fear Allah and do right, that will win (in the end)" (24:52) remarked to 'Umar bin al-Khaṭṭāb "indeed Allah has compressed in this verse whatever was revealed to 'Īsā concerning the states of this world and the hereafter."[2]

Another example of this unique concise comprehensiveness of the Qur'ānic verses is the following verse: "So We sent this inspiration to the mother of Moses: 'Suckle (thy child)'" (28:7). In this one verse, there are simultaneously mentioned two commands, two prohibitions and two glad tidings given to the mother of Prophet Mūsā (AS).[3]

Another example of extreme brevity, yet full of meaning is the verse "In the Law of Equality there is (saving of) Life to you" (2:179) which provides a sharp contrast to the famous phrase known among the Arabs: "murder is more deterrent for murder".

Among the forms of brevity is included a unique kind of ellipticism which is self-evident and free from confusion despite omission. And the most frequent of these omissions is where somebody's statement is dispensed with. The most brilliant example of this is reflected in the verse: "(They will be) in Gardens (of Delight): they will question each other, And (ask) of the Sinners: What led you into Hell Fire?" (74:40-42).

The verse refers to the inmates of Paradise who will be talking about the condition of the criminals. Some of those who would know of their condition will be asking about them saying "what conducted you to the Hell?"

Another form of ellipticism is the omission of the attributive clause, as in the verse "but it is righteousness – to believe in Allah" (2:177)

---

1 Maḥmūd bin 'Umar al-Zamakhsharī, *al-Kashshāf*, 6: 262.

2 'Ayyāḍ (sic) bin Mūsā al-Yaḥṣubī, *Kitāb al-Shifā' bi Ta'rīf Ḥuqūq al-Muṣṭafā*, 1: 200.

3 Ibid.

At times, a whole sentence is omitted when the context points to its assumed status in the speech like in the verse: "Then We told Moses by inspiration: 'Strike the sea with thy rod', So it divided" (26:63) the presumed sentence is *fa ḍaraba fanfalaqa*: "so he struck and it was set apart".

These forms include a sentence which informs about a particular matter in such a way that it covers not only that particular matter but also other things. In this way, the following purposes are attained: the general injunction, the particular injunction and the added sense that the particular matter covered by that particular injunction belongs to the category of the general injunction.

10.2. Habits of the Qur'ān

It is the function of a scholar of the Qur'ān to familiarize himself with the habits of the Qur'ān through a reflection on its words and vocabulary. Some of the early scholars have dealt with this aspect of the Qur'ānic studies. For example, Ibn 'Abbās is reported to have said: 'every cup (*ka's*) in the Qur'ān means wine'.[1] It has been reported in the *Ṣaḥīḥ* of al-Bukhārī that Ibn 'Uyaynah said: 'the word *maṭar* (rain) has always been used in the Qur'ān in the sense of punishment, while for the rain the Arabs employed the word: *ghayth* as the Qur'ān says: "He is the One that sends down rain (even) after (men) have given up all hope" (42:28).[2]

Also, it is reported that Ibn 'Abbās said "wherever the words (O people) occur, then this is an address to the polytheists of Makkah."[3]

Al-Jāḥiẓ says in his work: *al-Bayān wa al-Tabyīn* "in the Qur'ān, there are certain concepts that are seldom separated in mention like prayer and poor-due (*ṣalāt* and *zakāt*), fear and hunger, Paradise and

---

1 Muḥammad bin Jarīr al-Ṭabarī, *Jāmi' al-Bayān 'an Ta'wīl Āyy al-Qur'ān*, 8: 6885.

2 Muḥammad bin Ismā'īl al-Bukhārī, *Ṣaḥīḥ al-Bukhārī*, 797, immediately before ḥadīth no. 4648.

3 'Alī bin Aḥmad al-Wāḥidī, *Asbāb Nuzūl al-Qur'ān*, 20-21.

Fire, incentive and warning, the 'Immigrants' and 'Helpers', Jinnies and humans."[1] I may add to these concepts: gain and loss, heaven and earth.

Al-Zamakhsharī and Fakhr al-Dīn Rāzī also mention that it is a habit of the Qur'ān that no warning is ever mentioned without being followed by a promise and never a threat without glad tidings.[2] This is done in a style of digressive or intervening phrase to highlight the contrast.

Imām Fakhr al-Dīn Rāzī says, while explaining the verse "One day will Allah gather the messengers together" (5:109), "the habit of the Glorious Book is that when it speaks about many kinds of legal ordinances and religious injunctions, then it follows them with issues of theology, explanation of the past conditions of prophets and states of the hereafter so as to lay further stress on the foregoing mention of obligations and injunctions."[3]

I have also come across many habits in the terminology of the Qur'ān through my own inductive effort that I will be mentioning in their places in the course of this work. Among these habits is that when the personal pronoun *hā'ulā'* is mentioned without the subsequent noun, then this is a reference to the polytheists of Makkah. For example in the verse: "Yea, I have given the good things of this life to these (men) and their fathers" (43:29) and in the verse: "if these (their descendants) reject them, Behold! We shall entrust their charge to a new people who reject them not" (6:89), the personal pronouns (*hā'ulā'i*) refer to the Makkan polytheists.

Abū al-Bāqā' al-Kafawī in his work: *al-Kulliyyāt* has collected in the beginning of his chapters, some general connotations of the

1 'Amr bin Baḥr al-Jāḥiẓ, *al-Bayān wa al-Tabyīn*, 'Abd al-Salām Muḥammad Hārūn, ed. 7th ed. (Cairo: Maktabat al-Khānjī, 1418/1998), 1: 21.

2 Maḥmūd bin 'Umar al-Zamakhsharī, *al-Kashshāf*, 5: 211; Al-Fakhr al-Rāzī, *al-Tafsīr al-Kabīr*, 28: 247-48.

3 Al-Fakhr al-Rāzī, *al-Tafsīr al-Kabīr*, 12: 121-22.

Qur'ānic vocabulary.[1] *Al-Itqān* by al-Suyūṭī also contains something of that information.[2]

The third aspect of inimitability is the knowledge and wisdom contained in it. It should be borne in mind that the sole fund of knowledge possessed by the Arabs consisted in their poetical heritage. 'Umar bin al-Khaṭṭāb (may God be pleased with him) had said: "poetry represented all their knowledge and nothing to them was more authentic."[3]

The Qur'ān contained two kinds of knowledge. One of them related to the history of past peoples, prophets, their missions and the positive or negative response that they received from their respective peoples. This kind of knowledge had been a preserve of only a few exceptional men among the Jews and Christians. But the Arabs had not been familiar with it. Therefore, when these facts of history were revealed in the Qur'ān, this provided ample testimony for the truthfulness of the Prophet (peace be upon him) and for the Divine origin of the Qur'ān. For example, the Qur'ān narrated the events relating to Mūsā and Khaḍir, Yūsuf and his brothers, people of the Cave, Dhul-Qarnayn and Luqmān. This kind of knowledge was such that everyone easily grasped when it was revealed in the Qur'ān.

The second kind of knowledge revealed in the Qur'ān consisted of those matters that required an understanding of the principles whereby its reality could be discerned by those gifted with intellectual skills. Further, it depended on the gradual progress of human knowledge to reveal itself to the minds who are capable of grasping this knowledge.

The presence of both the above kinds of knowledge in the Qur'ān was unmistakable evidence that this Book was revealed by Allah to a

---

1 Abū al-Baqā' Ayyūb bin Mūsā al-Ḥusaynī al-Kafawī, *al-Kulliyyāt: Mu'jam fī al-Muṣṭalaḥāt wa al-Furūq al-Lughawiyyah*, 'Adnān Darwīsh & Muḥammad al-Miṣrī, eds. (Beirut: Mu'assasat al-Risālah, 1412/1992).

2 Jalāl al-Dīn 'Abd al-Raḥmān al-Suyūṭī, *al-Itqān*, 1: 453-60.

3 Muḥammad bin Salām al-Jumaḥī, *Ṭabaqāt Fuḥūl al-Shu'arā'*, 22.

Prophet who was unlettered and who lived all his life among people who did not possess any such heritage in the past.

The fourth aspect of inimitability is that it contained news about unseen matters. For example, the Qur'ān predicted the victory of the Romans over the Persians in the chapter "the Romans". It had also predicted the conquest of Makkah two years before this event in the chapter "Victory".

However, the real basis of inimitability of the Qur'ān, according to the majority of scholars, remains its highest miraculous level of eloquence and rhetorical perfection. For this is the most regular and consistent feature of the Qur'ān that runs throughout this Book in all its chapters. Whereas the narration of past events, particular forms of knowledge, prediction of future events or news of unseen matters are found in some parts of the Qur'ān only. Therefore, it is the linguistic and literary aspect of this Book—an aspect that characterizes all its verses and chapters—which really constitutes the foundation of its miraculous nature. It is this aspect of Qur'ān's inimitability which has engaged the attention of the scholars of Rhetorics and Stylistics throughout history. These scholars have labored hard to demonstrate the miraculous status of this Book and have furnished in their works an incontrovertible evidence for it.

BIBLIOGRAPHY

Ibn ʻĀdil, Abū Ḥafṣ ʻUmar bin ʻAlī al-Ḥanbalī, *al-Lubāb fī ʻUlūm al-Kitāb*, ʻĀdil Ahmad ʻĀbd al-Mawjūd et al., eds. (Beirut: Dār al-Kutub al-ʻIlmiyyah, 1419/1998).

Al-Ālūsī, Abūal-Faḍl Shihāb al-Dīn al-Sayyid Maḥmūd, *Rūḥ al-Maʻānī fī Tafsīr al-Qur'ān al-ʻAẓīm wa al-Sabʻ al-Mathānī*, Muḥammad Aḥmad al-Amad and ʻUmar ʻAbd al-Salām al-Salāmī, eds. (Beirut: Dār Iḥyā' al-Turāth al-ʻArabī and Mu'assasat al-Ta'rīkh al-ʻArabī, 1420/1999).

Ibn al-ʻArabī, al-Qāḍī Abū Bakr Muḥammad bin ʻAbd Allāh, *Aḥkām al-Qur'ān*, ʻAlī Muḥammad al-Bajāwī, ed. (Beirut: Dār al-Maʻrifah li al-Ṭibāʻah wa al-Nashr, n.d.).

____, *ʻĀriḍat al-Aḥwadhī*, Ṣidqī Jamīl al-ʻAṭṭār, ed. (Beirut: Dār al-Fikr li al-Ṭibāʻah wa al-Nashr wa al-Tawzīʻ, 1425-26/2005).

____, *Kitāb al-ʻAwāsim min al-Qawāṣim*, ʻAbd al-Ḥamīd bin Bādīs, ed. (n.p.: al-Maṭbaʻah al-Jazā'iriyyah al-Islāmiyyah, 1345/1926).

Al-Aṣfahānī, Abū al-Qāsim al-Ḥusayn bin Muḥammad al-Rāghib, *al-Mufradāt fī Gharīb al-Qur'ān*, Muḥammad Sayyid Kaylānī, ed. (Beirut: Dār al-Maʻrifah, n.d.).

Al-ʻAsqalānī, Aḥmad bin ʻAlī bin Ḥajar, *Fatḥ al-Bārī Sharḥ Ṣaḥīḥ al-Bukhārī* (Riyadh: Dār al-Salām, 1418/1998).

Ibn ʻAṭiyyah, ʻAbd al-Ḥaqq bin Ghālib al-Andalusī, *al-Muḥarrir al-Wajīz fī Tafsīr al-Kitāb al-ʻAzīz*, ʻAbd Allāh bin Ibrāhīm al-Anṣārī and ʻAbd al-ʻĀl al-Sayyid Ibrāhīm, eds., 2nd ed. (n.p.: n.p., n.d.).

Al-Baghawī, Abū Muḥammad al-Ḥusayn bin Masʻūd, *Maʻālim al-Tanzīl*, Khālid ʻAbd al-Raḥmān al-ʻAkk and Marwān Sawār, eds. (Beirut: Dār al-Maʻrifah, n.d.).

Al-Bāqillānī, Abū Bakr bin al-Ṭayyib, *al-Intiṣār li al-Qur'ān*, Muḥammad ʻIṣām al-Quḍāt, ed. (Amman & Beirut: Dār al-Fatḥ li al-Nashr wa al-Tawzīʻ & Dār Ibn Ḥazm li al-Ṭibāʻah wa al-Nashr wa al-Tawzīʻ, 1422/2001).

Al-Bayḍāwī, ‘Abd Allāh bin ‘Umar bin Muḥammad al-Shīrāzī, *Anwār al-Tanzīl wa Asrār al-Ta’wīl al-Ma‘rūf bi Tafsīr al-Bayḍāwī* (n.p.: Dār al-Jīl, 1329 AD).

Al-Bukhārī, ‘Abd al-‘Azīz, *Kashf al-Asrār Sharḥ ‘alā Uṣūl al-Bazdawī* (Beirut: Dār al-Kutub al-‘Ilmiyyah, 1997).

Al-Bukhārī, Muḥammad bin Ismā‘īl, *Ṣaḥīḥ al-Bukhārī* (Riyadh: Dār al-Salām, 1419/1999).

Al-Dānī, Abū ‘Amr al-Andalusī, *al-Bayān fī ‘Add Āyy al-Qur’ān*, ed., Ghānim Qudūrī al-Ḥamad (Kuwait: Markaz al-Makhṭūṭāt wa al-Turāth, 1414/1994).

Al-Dāwūdī, Muḥammad bin ‘Alī bin Aḥmad, *Ṭabaqāt al-Mufassirīn* (Beirut: Dār al-Kutub al-‘Ilmiyyah, n.d.).

Al-Fārisī, Abū ‘Alī al-Ḥasan bin ‘Abd al-Ghaffār, *al-Ḥujjah li al-Qurrā’ al-Sab‘ah*, Badr al-Dīn Qahwajī and Bashīr Juwayjātī, eds. (Damascus & Beirut: Dār al-Ma’mūn li al-Turāth, 1404/1984-1419/1999).

Al-Fayrūzābādī, Muḥammad bin Ya‘qūb, *Baṣā’ir Dhawī al-Tamyīz fī Laṭā’if al-Kitāb al-‘Azīz*, Muḥammad ‘Alī al-Najjār, ed. (Beirut: Dār al-Kutub al-‘Ilmiyyah, n.d.).

Al-Ghazālī, Abū Ḥāmid, *Faḍā’iḥ al-Bāṭiniyyah*, ‘Abd al-Raḥmān Badawī, ed. (Cairo: al-Dār al-Qawmiyyah li al-Ṭibā‘at wa al-Nashr, 1383/1964).

____, *Iḥyā’ ‘Ulūm al-Dīn* (n.p.: Maktabah wa Maṭba‘ah Karyāṭah Fūtarā, n.d.).

Al-Ḥākim, Muḥammad bin ‘Abd Allāh, *al-Mustadrak ‘alā al-Ṣaḥīḥayn*, Maḥmūd Maṭrajī, ed. (Beirut: Dār al-Fikr, 1421/2001).

Ibn Ḥanbal, Aḥmad bin Muḥammad, *al-Musnad*, Aḥmad Muḥammad Shākir and Ḥamzah Aḥmad al-Zayn, eds. (Cairo: Dār al-Ḥadīth, 1416/1995).

Abū Ḥayyān Muḥammad bin Yūsuf, *Tafsīr al-Baḥr al-Muḥīṭ* (Beirut: Dār al-Fikr li al-Ṭibā‘ah wa al-Nashr wa al-Tawzī‘, 1403/1983).

Al-Jāḥīẓ, ‘Amr bin Baḥr, *al-Bayān wa al-Tabyīn*, ‘Abd al-Salām Muḥammad Hārūn, ed. 7th ed. (Cairo: Maktabat al-Khānjī, 1418/1998).

Ibn al-Jazarī, Muḥammad bin Muḥammad bin ‘Alī bin Yūsuf, *Manẓūmat al-Jazariyyah* (n.p.: Shu‘bat Taw‘iyat al-Jāliyāt bi al-Zulfā, n.d.).

Ibn Jinnī, Abū al-Fatḥ ‘Uthmān, *al-Khaṣā’iṣ*, Muḥammad ‘Alī al-Najjār, ed. (Cairo: Maṭba‘at Dār al-Kutub al-Miṣriyyah, 1371/1952).

____, *Sirr Ṣanā'at al-I'rāb*, Ḥasan Handāwī, ed. (Damascus: Dār al-Qalam, 1405/1985).

Al-Jurjānī, 'Abd al-Qāhir, *Kitāb Dalā'il al-I'jāz fī 'Ilm al-Ma'ānī*, Muḥammad 'Abduhū et al., eds. (n.p.: Dār al-Manār, 1367 AH).

Al-Jumaḥī, Muḥammad bin Salām, *Ṭabaqāt Fuḥūl al-Shu'arā'*, Maḥmūd Muḥammad Shākir, ed. (n.p.: Dār al-Ma'ārif li al-Ṭibā'ah wa al-Nash, n.d.).

Al-Jurjānī, al-Sayyid al-Sharīf 'Alī bin Muḥammad bin 'Alī al-Ḥusaynī, *al-Ḥāshiyah 'alā Kitāb al-Kashshāf* (n.p.: Sharikat Maktabat wa Maṭba'at Muṣṭafā al-Bābī al-Ḥalabī wa Awlāduh, 1385/1966).

____, *al-Miṣbāḥ fī Sharḥ al-Miftāḥ*, Yūksal Jalīk, ed. (unpublished PhD thesis, Marmara University, Turkey, 2009).

Al-Juwaynī, 'Abd al-Malik bin 'Abd Allāh bin Yūsuf, *al-Burhān fī Uṣūl al-Fiqh*, 'Abd al-'Aẓīm al-Dīb, ed. (Doha: Maṭābi' al-Dawḥah al-Ḥadīthah, 1399 AH).

Al-Kafawī, Abū al-Baqā' Ayyūb bin Mūsā al-Ḥusaynī, *al-Kulliyyāt: Mu'jam fī al-Muṣṭalaḥāt wa al-Furūq al-Lughawiyyah*, 'Adnān Darwīsh & Muḥammad al-Miṣrī, eds. (Beirut: Mu'assasat al-Risālah, 1412/1992).

Ibn Kathīr, Ismā'īl, *al-Sīrah al-Nabawiyyah*, Muṣṭafā 'Abd al-Wāḥid, ed. (Beirut: Dār al-Ma'rifah li al-Ṭibā'ah wa al-Nashr, 1396/1976).

Al-Khandawī, Muḥammad Ismā'īl, *al-Aqwāl al-Imdādiyyah 'alā Muqaddimat al-Jazariyyah bi al-Su'āl wa al-Jawāb* (Lahore: al-Maktabah al-Imdādiyyah al-Tajwīdiyyah, 1394/1974).

Mālik bin Anas, *al-Muwaṭṭa'*, Muḥammad Fu'ād 'Abd al-Bāqī, ed. (Beirut: Dār Iḥyā' al-Turāth al-'Arabī, n.d.).

Ibn Manẓūr, Muḥammad bin Mukarram, *Lisān al-'Arab* (Qum: Nashr Adab al-Ḥawzah, 1405 AH).

Al-Māzarī, Muḥammad bin 'Alī bin 'Umar bin Muḥammad al-Tamīmī, *Īḍāḥ al-Maḥṣūl min Burhān al-Uṣūl*, 'Ammār al-Ṭālibī, ed. (n.p.: Dār al-Gharb al-Islāmī, n.d.).

Al-Mubarrid, Muḥammad bin Yazīd, *al-Kāmil*, Muḥammad Aḥmad al-Dālī, ed. (Beirut: Mu'assasat al-Risālah, 1406/1986).

Ibn al-Nujaym, Zayn al-Dīn, *al-Baḥr al-Rā'iq Sharḥ Kanz al-Daqā'iq* (Quetta: al-Maktabah al-Mājidiyyah, n.d.).

Al-Qaysī, Makkī bin Abī Ṭālib, *Kitāb al-Kashf 'an Wujūh al-Qirā'āt al-Sab' wa 'Ilalihā wa Ḥijajihā*, Muḥyi al-Dīn Ramaḍān, ed., 2nd ed. (Beirut: Mu'assasat al-Risālah, 1401/1981).

Al-Qurṭubī, Muḥammad bin Aḥmad, *al-Jāmi' li Aḥkām al-Qur'ān*, Ṣadqī Muḥammad Jamīl and 'Irfān al-'Ashshā, eds. (Beirut: Dār al-Fikr, 1414/1993).

Al-Qushayrī, Muslim bin al-Ḥajjāj bin Muslim, *Ṣaḥīḥ Muslim* (Riyadh: Dār al-Salām, 1419/1998).

Al-Rāzī, al-Fakhr, *al-Tafsīr al-Kabīr* (Cairo: Mu'assasat al-Maṭbū'āt al-Islāmiyyah, n.d.).

Ibn Rushd, Abū al-Walīd al-Andalusī, *al-Bayān wa al-Taḥṣīl wa al-Sharḥ wa al-Tawjīh wa al-Ta'līl fī Masā'il al-Mustakhrajah*, Muḥammad Ḥajjī, ed., 2nd ed. (Beirut: Dār al-Gharb al-Islāmī, 1408/1988)

____, *Faṣl al-Maqāl fīmā bayn al-Ḥikmah wa al-Sharī'at min al-Ittiṣāl*, Muḥammad 'Amārah, ed. (Cairo: Dār al-Ma'ārif, n.d.).

Al-Sijistānī, Abū Dāwūd Sulaymān bin al-Ash'ath, *Kitāb al-Maṣāḥif*, ed. Arthur Jeffery (n.p.: al-Maṭba'at al-Raḥmāniyyah, 1355/1936).

____, Abū Dāwūd Sulaymān bin al-Ash'ath, *Sunan Abī Dāwūd* (Riyadh: Dār al-Salām, 1420/1999).

Al-Sakkākī, Yūsuf bin Abī Bakr Muḥammad bin 'Alī, *Miftāḥ al-'Ulūm*, Na'īm Zarūr, ed. (Beirut: Dār al-Kutub al-'Ilmiyyah, 1403/1983).

Al-Ṣan'ānī, 'Abd al-Razzāq bin Hammām, *al-Muṣannaf*, Ḥabīb al-Raḥmān al-A'ẓamī ed. (Johannesburg: Majlis Ilmi, 1392/1972).

Al-Sayālkawtī, 'Abd al-Ḥakīm, *Ḥāshiyat al-'Allāmah 'Abd al-Ḥakīm al-Sayālkawtī 'alā al-Tafsīr li al-Qāḍī al-Bayḍāwī* (Quetta: Maktabah Islāmiyyah, n.d.).

Al-Shāṭibī, Ibrāhīm bin Mūsā, *al-Mawāfaqāt fī Uṣūl al-Sharī'ah*, 'Abd Allāh Darāz, ed., 2nd ed. (Beirut: Dār al-Ma'rifah li al-Ṭibā'ah wa al-Nashr, 1395/1975).

Ibn Abī Shaybah, 'Abd Allāh bin Muḥammad, *al-Muṣannaf*, Muḥammad 'Awwāmah, ed. (Beirut: Dār Qurtubah li al-Tibā'at wa al-Nashr wa al-Tawzī', 1427/2006).

Al-Subkī, 'Alī bin 'Abd al-Kāfī and 'Abd al-Wahhāb bin 'Alī, *al-Ibhāj fī Sharḥ al-Minhāj*, Aḥmad Jamāl al-Zamzamī and Nūr al-Dīn 'Abd al-Jabbār Ṣaghīrī, eds. (Dubai: Dār al-Buḥūth li al-Dirāsāt al-Islāmiyyah wa Iḥyā' al-Turāth, 1424/2004).

Al-Suyūṭī, 'Abd al-Raḥmān bin Abī Bakr, *al-Durr al-Manthūr fī al-Tafsīr bi al-Ma'thūr* (Beirut: Dār al-Kutub al-'Ilmiyyah, 1421/2000).

____, *al-Itqān fī 'Ulūm al-Qur'ān*, Muṣṭafā Dīb al-Bughā, ed. (Beirut: Dār Ibn Kathīr, 1407/1987).

____, *al-Itqān fī 'Ulūm al-Qur'ān*, Muḥammad Abū al-Faḍl Ibrāhīm, ed. (Cairo: al-Hay'ah al-Miṣriyyah al-'Āmmah li al-Kitāb, 1974).

Al-Ṭabarī, Muḥammad bin Jarīr, *Jāmi' al-Bayān 'an Ta'wīl Āyy al-Qur'ān*, Aḥmad Abd al-Razzāq al-Bakrī, et al., eds. (Cairo: Dār al-Salām li al-Ṭibā'ah wa al-Nashr wa al-Tawzī' wa al-Tarjumah, 1429/2008).

Al-Taftāzānī, Mas'ūd bin 'Umar, *Sharḥ al-Maqāṣid*, 'Abd al-Raḥmān 'Umayrah, ed. (Beirut: 'Ālam al-Kutub, 1419/1998).

____, *Sharḥ al-Talwīh 'alā al-Tawḍīḥ* (n.p.: Dār al-'Ahd al-Jadīd li al-Ṭibā'ah, n.d.).

Ibn Abī Ṭālib, 'Alī, *Nahj al-Balāghah*, Muḥammad al-Raḍī bin al-Ḥasan al-Mūsawī, comp., Muḥammad 'Abduhū, comm., Muḥammad Muḥyi al-Dīn 'Abd al-Ḥamīd, ed. (n.p.: Maṭba'at al-Istiqāmah, n.d.).

Ṭāsh Kubrā Zādah, Aḥmad bin Muṣṭafā, *Muftāh (sic) al-Sa'ādah wa Miṣbāh al-Siyādah fī Mawḍū'āt al-'Ulūm* (Beirut: Dār al-Kutub al-'Ilmiyyah, 1405/1985).

Al-Ṭībī, Sharaf al-Dīn al-Ḥusayn bin 'Abd Allāh, *Futūḥ al-Ghayb 'an Kashf Qinā' al-Rayb* [from the beginning to *Sūrat al-Shu'arā'*], a number of researchers, eds. (MA & PhD Theses, al-Jāmi'ah al-Islāmiyyah, al-Madīnat al-Munawwarah, 1413-16 AH).

Al-Tirmidhī, Muḥammad bin 'Īsā, *Jāmi' al-Tirmidhī* (Riyadh: Dār al-Salām, 1420/1999).

Al-Wāḥidī, 'Alī bin Aḥmad, *Asbāb Nuzūl al-Qur'ān*, al-Sayyid Aḥmad Ṣaqar, ed. (n.p.: Dār al-Kitāb al-Jadīd, 1389/1969).

Al-Yaḥṣubī, 'Ayyāḍ bin Mūsā, *Kitāb al-Shifā' bi Ta'rīf Ḥuqūq al-Muṣṭafā*, Kamāl Basyūnī Zaghlūl al-Miṣrī, ed., 3rd ed. (Beirut: Mu'assasat al-Kutub al-Thaqāfiyyah, n.d.).

____, *Tartīb al-Madārik wa Taqrīb al-Masālik li Ma'rifat Madhhab Mālik*,

Muḥammad Sālim Hāshim, ed. (Beirut: Dār al-Kutub al-'Ilmiyyah, 1418/1998).

Al-Zabīdī, Muḥammad Murtaḍā al-Ḥusaynī, *Tāj al-'Urūs min Jawāhir al-Qāmūs*, Ḥusayn Naṣṣār, ed. (n.p.: Maṭba'at Ḥukūmat al-Kuwayt, 1394/1974).

Al-Zamakhsharī, Maḥmūd bin 'Umar, *al-Kashshāf 'an Ḥaqā'iq Ghawāmiḍ al-Tanzīl wa 'Uyūn al-Aqāwīl fī Wujūh al-Ta'wīl*, 'Ādil Aḥmad 'Abd al-Mawjūd and 'Alī Muḥammad Mu'awwaḍ, eds. (Riyadh: Maktabat al-'Abīkān, 1418/1998).

Al-Zarkashī, Muḥammad bin 'Abd Allāh, *al-Burhān fī 'Ulūm al-Qur'ān*, Muḥammad Abū al-Faḍl Ibrāhīm, ed., 2nd ed. (Beirut: Dār al-Ma'rifah li al-Ṭibā'ah wa al-Nashr, n.d.).

Al-Zarqānī, Muḥammad 'Abd al-'Aẓīm, *Manāhil al-'Irfān fī 'Ulūm al-Qur'ān* (Beirut: Dār al-Fikr, 1424/2004).

Al-Ziriklī, Khayr al-Dīn, *al-A'lām*, 5th ed. (Beirut: Dār al-'Ilm li al-Malāyīn, 1980).

Zuhayr bin Abī Salmā, *Dīwān Zuhayr bin Abī Salmā*, 'Alī Ḥasan Fā'ūr, ed. (Beirut: Dār al-Kutub al-'Ilmiyyah, 1408/1988).

Al-Zujāj, *I'rāb al-Qur'ān*, Ibrāhīm al-Abyārī, ed. (Cairo: al-Hay'at al-'Āmmah li Shu'ūn al-Maṭābi' al-Amīriyyah, 1963 AD).